"Amy continues to take us on a journey of her life with its ups and the downs. I have known Amy on a personal level for the past 35 years and have enjoyed the passion that she has for life and the love of family. I think that almost everyone can say that life doesn't always go your way but it is how you handle the situation that will set you apart. Amy has a unique way of showing us how to rise above—I would encourage you to pick up this book—as we can all use a little more enrichment on living your best life."

—Darlene Nowak-Baker

"In *A Little Me,* you'll gain some raw insight into the life experiences, family, and faith that shaped the Amy Roloff we have all grown to love. Amy weaves her personal story around differences and commonality, and challenges us along the way to be confident in our own unique purpose. Read this book, and find a little more encouragement to be a lot more you!"

—Chester Goad
Author, speaker & host of "The Leaderbyte" podcast

"Amy fearlessly shares her private stories with us – from her challenging childhood to leaving home to marry, to her hit family tv series and marriage struggles and from her divorce journey leading into her unexpected blossoming second act. This is a truly inspirational memoir."

—Lisa Dixon
Health insurance broker and business entrepreneur

"Amy Roloff's *A Little Me* is an inspirational book that was hard to put down. Whether you or someone you know has a challenge to overcome, you will find Amy's story one that gives you the hope and faith to face anything! As a mom of a quadriplegic, I love Amy's statement that "different makes people uncomfortable. Most people are not sure how to act, react, or feel around others who are physically different." This hit home for me! We need to realize that people that are "different" are just like us in so many ways! You'll be surprised when you leave YOUR comfort zone and befriend someone that is physically different!"

—LeAnn Sullivan
Thrive Ministries Director, Southern Idaho Ministry Network

"This is the tale of courageous Amy Roloff - as told in her own words. Amy has in life been a Michigander, a daughter and sister, a wife, a mother, a reality television star, a fundraiser and now a writer. Across these pages Amy shares her personal memories and thoughts, written as she boldly faces the future with a resilient, open heart. This is a powerful story about a faithful spirit."

—Jack Morrissey
Producer, Disney's Beauty and the Beast

A Little *Me*

A Little

Me

Amy Roloff

Editors: Hamishe Randall, Jackson Haynes, and Regina Cornell

Cover Design: 3SIXTY Marketing Studio - 3sixtyprinting.com

Interior Design: 3SIXTY Marketing Studio - 3sixtyprinting.com

Indigo River Publishing
3 West Garden Street, Ste. 352
Pensacola, FL 32502
www.indigoriverpublishing.com

Ordering Information:

Quantity sales: Special discounts are available on quantity purchases by corporations, associations, and others. For details, contact the publisher at the address above.

Orders by US trade bookstores and wholesalers: Please contact the publisher at the address above.

Printed in the United States of America

Library of Congress Control Number: 2019941374

ISBN: 978-1-948080-84-2

First Edition

With Indigo River Publishing, you can always expect great books, strong voices, and meaningful messages.
Most importantly, you'll always find . . . words worth reading.

To my dad and mom, Gordon and Patricia,
for all your love, encouragement, and support when I
needed it most, and every day of my life.
I'm so thankful for you both.
You've always made me feel I could shine in all I do.

To my four kids, Jeremy, Zachary, Molly, and Jacob:
You each inspire me to be the best I can be as a mom and
as a person every day. You are my greatest gifts in life.
Love you forever and always.

Prologue

A Little Me

A month before Christmas Eve, the church I attended with my family growing up was planning to recreate a live manger scene in front of the church before each of the three services that evening. They reached out to the youth and others in the church to see who wanted to be a part of it.

When I heard about it, I hesitated to let my parents know. Although I wanted to take part, I was really uncertain and nervous to even think I might have a chance. The live nativity scene wouldn't have any speaking parts; it would simply be a wonderful live visual presentation depicting the story of Christmas, the birth of Jesus. It wasn't typical for me to get excited about putting myself out there, but this was a perfect opportunity for me to go for something I really wanted. Even back then, it was hard just to take baby steps outside of my box—that box about being different and hoping no one would notice. I was going to give it a try regardless of what I thought others would think or how scared I was.

I was about eleven years old, and already I knew when you look different on the outside, beauty takes on a whole different meaning, which speaks volumes in other's perception of you. Worrying no one would think of me as worthy or beautiful made me hesitate about so many things; my difference in being a little person got in the way.

This time I decided to get outside of that not-good-enough box and take the risk. I told my parents about the live nativity event and said I wanted to put my name on the list to try out for a part.

Why this time? I had tried out for several parts in plays and solo parts in choir at school and church, but never got them. Instead, I always seemed to be cast in the choir or as part of the "crowd" scenes. In the back of my mind, I often thought I didn't get the part because

I was different. I didn't think that maybe others had more talent or were just better for the parts. Even then, I subconsciously let being different become a possible reason for not getting what I went after. I didn't use being different as an excuse, but it more or less gave me a reason why some things didn't go the way I wanted them to.

My parents always encouraged and supported me to go after whatever I wanted to do and often told me not to ever think or let others tell me I can't. I remember my father telling me I have to always keep trying and not give up. As long as you keep trying, you just never know when the moment will be that it all comes together. Don't create a reason to complain about or say you can't do something. The only person I have to point at when I decide to give up or not to try is myself. The only person who can come up with an excuse for why I may not succeed at something is myself. As my father often told me, I just have to go out there and do my best; it's all I can ask of myself. Even if I don't always get what I want, that doesn't mean I shouldn't keep trying. You'll never know if you don't try.

So I put my name on the list to be Mary or the angel in the live nativity scene. I told my parents when I needed to be at the tryouts, planning meetings, and work events. I was hoping to show everyone I was willing and able to help build the stable scene, set up for the nativity, and do what I could regardless of what happened. If they saw me helping out with the other youth, then maybe they would see no reason why I couldn't be Mary or the angel or any other role in the live nativity. I wanted to know how it felt to go after something I wanted and to succeed.

Of course, others wanted to take part in the Christmas Eve nativity event as well, and I waited anxiously to see if I would be chosen for a role. My thoughts turned to doubts that I probably wouldn't be, because I usually didn't get chosen. Even though I tried, part of me always felt as if I would never be good enough or be seen as good enough because I was different, a little person. I used the thought of not being good enough almost as a safeguard so I wouldn't be as disappointed.

I didn't doubt myself because I thought I couldn't do it, but rather because I was different, and *different* makes people uncomfortable and uncertain. Many people aren't sure how to act, react, or feel around others who are physically different than themselves. I've never understood why others would feel this way about me, but I guess it's a natural reaction for all of us sometimes. I often thought, *Okay, so I'm a dwarf.* So what? But it does affect people. How do I manage being a dwarf and the effect it has on others if I'm not even sure how it affects me?

When I got the news that I had gotten the part of the angel, I was so thrilled and excited. I couldn't believe it. My parents were thrilled for me too. They knew how much I wanted it and had worked for it. They knew it would be a confidence booster for me, and they were right.

The weather was cold, and snow flurries were coming down that Christmas Eve night. It reminded me of the actual Christmas story, when Joseph and Mary, riding on a donkey, were on the road going to Bethlehem. I had to be outside in the cold for about thirty minutes before each service. It didn't matter to me. I was just hoping the event wouldn't be canceled.

Being the angel meant I had to climb up on a ladder behind the stable scene so people could see me. *No problem,* I thought, but standing there for that long toward the top of a ladder made some people quite nervous, and they weren't as sure I could do it as I was. *No! I can do this,* I told myself. My father reassured them and asked them to give me a chance.

So there I stood as the angel in the Christmas story that told of the good news that a Savior was born. The snow was falling, the soft glow of a spotlight faintly shown on me, and the sparkle of twinkling lights around the nativity scene made me feel special—important—and a part of making this Christmas Eve special for everyone who came to church as well. It was worth standing on a ladder in the cold of the night for three services to help make this significant yet simple story come to life. It meant the world to me that I had gone for something that was scary, something I wanted, and got it. It was a glorious Christmas Eve night.

Whether it was just a simple part in a live nativity event as a young girl or other dreams I had later on, such as learning how to cook, I had to find it within myself to go after what I wanted. I just had to take a chance, give it a try, and keep trying. It would be a lesson I would go back to over and over again throughout my life—there are always two possible outcomes: failure or success. Always keep trying because you just never know if you'll succeed if you don't try.

Growing up, we typically have many lofty dreams and aspirations, and wonder as the days, months, and years go by if any of them will come true. I did dream a lot! Would any of the dreams I had ever come to fruition, or were the challenges too big and success—what I thought of as success—too far out of reach? Would the hero ever be me, or would it always be someone else? Was this just the way life was going to be when you are different?

A Little Me

I hoped I would be a mom one day, go on mission trips, and help others and make a difference in people's lives. Maybe own my own restaurant, be a singer, a teacher, a musician, a chef, own my own B&B—my imagination and dreams were unlimited. However, to make dreams come true we need to go after them. They won't just magically come true if we don't take action.

The one dream I never had was To Be Tall. That was something I knew could never happen, and why aspire to be something without the remotest possibility of becoming reality? I looked at the opportunities that seemed to come easier for people who were tall or of average height. It wasn't always easy for me to believe in myself, to have determination and confidence, which I knew was going to be the big difference in having a good attitude and in anything I did in my life. Doubt couldn't be a part of the picture, but giving myself more positive affirmations needed to be, in order to get where I wanted to go. Someone *different* was usually not the hero in the books I read and the movies I saw. They were often small or temporary characters, at first touted as unique and special but soon forgotten because what good they might have done was fleeting in other people's perception since they didn't fit the mold of what a hero was.

With my family, my faith, and believing in myself that I matter, have value and a purpose, I could face the world as *different* and become my own hero.

This is the life, so far, of a little woman who got to experience some Big Things—things I never thought I would. As I reflect back on my life, I'm amazed at the challenges I've overcome and the things I've experienced, but also some things I didn't. All in all, my life has been a wonderful life. It would be quite boring if everything in life went perfectly smoothly. How would we truly learn and grow, push ourselves, and have the sweet taste of success without failure?

I was brought up to believe we are all meant for a purpose and to serve. Now it is my job and goal to figure out what I'm meant to do and how I can serve.

CHAPTER 1

Uniquely Made

When you are "different," life feels limited and unpredictable, even more so than I imagine it does for others. You get this vibe that there is a lot you can't do, but you can also sense what you are more than capable of accomplishing. I was unsure of my capabilities because I was a dwarf, a little person. It was a subtle thing I picked up from others or that I simply felt, and it was a big part of what I thought growing up, getting *can* and *can't* all mixed up.

It wasn't that I thought I couldn't do certain things, but rather that I thought others saw me as incapable. I made assumptions and had expectations about my life based on having dwarfism, and felt that others did as well. The big question: Was I letting others make me feel lessened, or were my own thoughts already doing it?

When people first saw me they probably thought, *What a hard and maybe sad life she has. She's short and doesn't look like me. She's different. What is she going to be able to do? She can hardly reach anything with her short arms and legs. She looks and walks funny. How old is she? She looks like a young kid* (when I might have been fifteen years old). Sometimes people said things to me out loud, and other times their body language spoke volumes. Stereotypes were thrown at me, and I was expected to live in a way others imagined for me.

But our lives don't have to follow others' preconceptions. People have that power only if we let them. Instead, always believe that you matter and have value, and find out for yourself what your life's purpose is. By the way, I'm still figuring that out because my life has changed, either as a result of my own choices or because of personal events. But in the end, everyone has a purpose.

Many people may seem to have an opinion about your life and may sometimes say what they think you can or cannot do. "That may be too difficult for you." And so they try to push you toward something easier and safer. When we hear those things often enough, we start believing them. We start believing that some of these perceived limitations are actual limitations! I admit, at times I would often fall into the "well, I can't do much about being a dwarf, so I might as well let life happen" mode of thinking.

When I thought others had doubts, I wanted to say out loud, *Why*? When I thought others ignored me I wanted to say even louder, *You know I'm right here, don't you?* When others made fun of me, I just wanted to hide underneath a rock. The older I got, how people approached me and what they said to me became subtler. Often, when I thought people were talking to me, I realized they were using me for attention or really just wanted to talk to the person I was with. I was usually a part of something, the conversation or the moment, but not really as myself. I felt more like an afterthought, or someone needed just for the moment, only to later be brushed aside.

You may know me from the hit reality TV show *Little People, BIG World* on TLC. We have filmed fourteen seasons of the show already. If you have seen the show, you may say, "I know her." I would respond back and say yes, yes you do. You've had a glimpse of who Amy Roloff is. But there is a lot you don't know. This is a little of my story—how I overcame the obstacles I faced, my own insecurities, a childhood illness, and the challenges of adulthood to get where I am today. Frankly, I'm amazed at how far I have come.

I've heard people say that I must have had a hard and kind of a sad life being different. Why? I've never quite understood that thinking. I definitely knew I was different from everyone around me, at least physically, and would face more challenges; but I got a little confidence now and again, enough to prove to myself that I could do anything I wanted to do. Just maybe others would see I could do more than they thought I could.

Yes, I'm different, but we're all different. Embrace that difference—you can excel because of it. Appreciate it and use it to your advantage instead of hiding and being afraid of it. I didn't do such a great job of appreciating my differences in my earlier years, and that laid a foundation of insecurity, a lack of confidence and self-worth, that wasn't the best to build my life upon. It wasn't easy, and I was often depressed, but over time I've learned how to overcome some of those insecurities and embrace and appreciate myself!

I was born with achondroplasia dwarfism. What? Yeah, I'm not a character like an Ewok in Star Wars or a munchkin in *The Wizard of Oz*. While I love both of these movies, what I didn't like was when people who had watched *The Wizard of Oz* would laugh and make fun of me and call me a munchkin, as if I were a character instead of a person. Often they would just keep going on and on in front of my friends or others. It would have been different if they had said these things privately, just to me, but being made fun of in front of other people made me feel less worthy as a person. I was not good at laughing at myself, brushing off the teasing and snide remarks, and moving on. It got to me sometimes, and I often took things a little too seriously.

About one in twenty-five thousand couples (for an average-size couple) has a chance of having an achondroplastic dwarf child. It's just a random mutation of the genes. So how am I different? Well, physically, I have shorter arms and legs, a regular-size torso, and a slightly larger head. But there are different variations of achondroplasia. In fact, there are hundreds of different kinds of dwarfism. All jokes aside, yes, I'm smart but not any smarter or less smart than anyone else because of my dwarfism. Okay, maybe I am just a little smarter than some. People would often tease me that I wasn't smart, and I think it took smarts to ignore that and believe in myself.

I realized early on that my physical appearance, what I look like on the outside, does matter. Whether we like it or not, the first impression we form about other people comes from their outward appearance. It's a fleeting moment of interaction. But maybe, just maybe, we'll take the time to have a conversation with them or get to know them first by other means before making a judgment about them. Getting past a physical difference is sometimes a hurdle to overcome.

I think back on all those first impressions and wonder how many people made snap judgments about me and failed to give me a chance because of my appearance, or how many opportunities I missed to maybe change their minds about me. And, man, that upsets me. Although I didn't want others to put so much emphasis on appearance, I did it myself and missed out on possible opportunities. Why? Because, growing up, my physical appearance mattered to me more than it should have. I wanted to fit in.

As I look back at pictures of my younger self, I had a pretty cute smile, blonde hair, and blue-green eyes, and I was physically fit. Yeah, I may have looked a little funny and ran a little differently, but I felt as if I could do anything and be anything. I just didn't feel as confident that others believed I could, and what they thought mattered more than it should have to me.

My parents always said I could do anything. So why is it that I don't remember myself as being very confident? I remember feeling easily intimidated by others and insecure. I seemed strong on the outside, but on the inside I was very shy and lonely, and felt scared about who I was and what I was really capable of doing. Frankly, I was a contradiction of thoughts and affirmations—*yes* and *no*, *can* and *can't*, *possible* and *impossible*. No wonder I was confused and spun myself in all different directions, afraid of failure and of pursuing success. It was much easier to maintain the status quo, not to mention more comfortable. It got me by.

I didn't have the kind of personality that would have allowed me to showcase or take advantage of being different. A lot of people will do certain things to try to be different, to gain that edge, that attention, to say, "Here I am. Look at me." Others who are different know how to take advantage of their differences to get what they want, to do what they want to do, and to become who they want to be in their community, group of friends, or work. They are the jokesters, the ones who can laugh at themselves, and so the big elephant in the room—being different—gets exposed and forgotten about as quickly as it was noticed. I wasn't one of these people.

Nope, not me. I didn't embrace myself and my environment as well as I wanted to. Sometimes I preferred to hide or blend in as part of the crowd. I didn't know how to be noticed without drawing too much attention to myself. It's probably why I was in awe of people who just naturally knew what to do in a crowd, how to make friends on the playground, how to take the initiative in college and risks at their work, and how to form relationships. They just seemed to know what they wanted to do and the people they wanted to be with, and weren't afraid and didn't let their differences get in the way. They took action regardless of what anyone thought about them.

It took much longer for me to figure this out. I often waited to be asked to be included and wasn't persistent in going after what

I wanted. I didn't take the initiative often enough. I didn't want to face rejection—the "no, we don't want you here" or "well, we're going on a long bike ride and we don't want you to slow us down; maybe next time" or "we've chosen someone else for the position with 'more qualifications' or who 'fits the position better.'" When something like that was said to me, I often took it to heart, and I took it a lot more seriously than I should have.

However, I always found a way to pick myself up and try again even though I thought, *No one really likes having me around,* or that I would never be good enough for a lot of things. I would need to find a way to do life differently on my own.

Being an achondroplastic dwarf made me different than those around me. Yet was I really *that* different than anyone else? I was in an average-size world, but I wasn't average size. I was different, but strangely not different enough. Even though I was able-bodied physically, by some I was considered disabled. I often didn't know what to do or how to think about myself and how I fit in the world around me. I sometimes felt stuck in the middle and didn't know which way to go. I was in this neutral zone, and sometimes I surprised myself when I actually went out on a limb and did something unexpected.

Now I had a choice in deciding who I was, what I wanted to do, what was possible or not, what my purpose was, why I mattered, and, frankly, if I was good enough. *Why am I waiting around for others to decide these things for me? Am I good enough? Can I or can't I?* I needed to do that for myself. I knew I needed to believe in and like myself. I needed to know within myself that I mattered, had value and a purpose.

I love the quote "Be yourself. Everyone else is already taken." Before I could really embrace this, which truly took me quite some time, I had to accept, appreciate, and value who I am first. I spent a lot of wasted time and energy looking for other people's approval and acceptance. I wasn't always comfortable being in my own skin, celebrating that there is only one of me, and isn't that fantastic? No one is just like me. If I couldn't believe in myself, then why would I expect others to accept and embrace me?

Maybe if I had stopped trying so hard to convince people to appreciate and accept me, and instead spent a little more precious time doing it for myself first, how much easier it would have been for others to see and embrace this different girl who just happens to be a dwarf. I mean, what a novel concept!

Encouragement from Amy:

~Just be yourself. There is only one unique, one-of-a-kind you, and you're the best at it. Everyone else is taken.

CHAPTER 2

Growing Up in an Average-Size Family

A Little Me

I can't imagine what my parents felt or thought when they found out their new baby girl was going to be different. They didn't know I was an achondroplastic dwarf until I was born. They definitely weren't expecting this kind of news. Why would they? No one else in the family had anything like this. They didn't have a wealth of information available to them back then—certainly not the overwhelming abundance of information we find on the Internet today—to be able to instantly look up everything they could about achondroplasia dwarfism. It was unknown territory.

What did this mean for them as parents? Had they done anything to cause this? Absolutely not. It was just a fluke genetic mutation that caused them to have a dwarf child. How would they parent a child that was different from their other two daughters, my older sisters? What kind of life would I have? Would they need to do anything special for me? How could they make my life a little easier, considering the challenges life would throw at me as I got older?

All my parents knew was they had a healthy baby girl. My two older sisters were going to have a baby sister to play with, to tease, to teach all about everything "girl." To tell her about boys and how to talk to them, about love, about friends, about what's cool and fashionable or not. To share thoughts and dreams with, to argue over time in the bathroom, clothes, and everything else sisters do.

I couldn't have asked for a better family. I was born and raised in Michigan in a suburb just outside of Detroit. My family lived in a typical middle-class neighborhood with nicely manicured lawns and front porches that many of the moms and dads would sit out on in the evenings as they watched the neighborhood kids playing in the street and riding bikes. It felt like the whole block was part of our own yard as well. Each house was one story with a basement, and similar to the one next door. The garage was in back with a yard big enough to play and hang out in with friends and have a barbecue. But my life wasn't all Norman Rockwell nostalgia; there were tough times growing up. However, we were a family living life with a daughter that was different, and this was our normal.

When I asked my mom and dad what their thoughts and feelings were when they heard the news that their baby girl was an achondroplastic dwarf, they said it took them by surprise at first. My mom was worried and uncertain about what to do. Would she be able to handle this? Would it be different to raise me than to raise my sisters? Was I going to be okay? My father was more matter-of-fact, practical, and confident. When challenges came up they would be able to handle them. Why worry about it now? They would raise me just like they were raising my older sisters, and later my younger brother. When my brother and I were older, he told me he often thought I got away with a lot and didn't get in trouble as he thought I should have sometimes. He was just jealous. We laugh about it now because he may be right.

Yep, they had the typical questions any new parents would have. Having a daughter who was different just came with a few extra layers to work through.

When I was born, my father saw I had ten fingers and ten toes and was physically perfect—meaning I could move my legs and arms, I was breathing, and I was healthy. He felt so proud and relieved when he saw me, but he also considered the future. What kind of future would I have? He comforted my mom in his practical way that all would be okay. "She may be different, but we'll raise her just like we have been doing with her sisters—with a lot of love. We'll help her be the best she can be." My dad may have wanted to fix everything, but he knew he couldn't fix this. Not that he wanted to, because there was nothing to fix about me. I was who I was. He was a man of faith and knew God would be watching over me.

I don't think anything is "typical" in any family when it comes to raising kids. Each family is unique. However, raising a child that was different from anyone else in their family and their community of friends was new territory that, for the most part, my parents were forging on their own. Being different was obvious to me growing up, but not because my parents or family made me feel that way. The physical environment around me didn't fit me, and so I began to see myself as *different* because of the experiences I had.

Kindergarten gave me my first experience of what would lie ahead in my school years and interacting with other kids.

I had to ride the bus with my sisters to school, which, at the time, seemed far away. It was hard to climb the few steps to get on the bus, but I did it. When I met the kids in my class, they weren't much different than I was. Many of them were a little taller, but a number of them were the same height as I was. They just looked a little more "average" than I did. Their arms and legs fit their bodies proportionally, whereas my arms and legs were shorter compared to my regular-size torso.

A little stool had been placed in the bathroom so I could reach the toilet and the sink. To me, this didn't seem weird or out of place, because I had the same thing in my house, only at home the stool stayed put, but at school it got moved around a lot and I didn't know where it went. Suddenly, the stool was for everyone, and often I'd go to the bathroom and it wouldn't be there. So each time I needed to go to the bathroom, I had to ask the teacher for the stool. I also used a stool underneath my desk to keep my feet from dangling and going to sleep.

Some of the kids would laugh at me and show off how they could reach things and didn't need a stool to help them. They laughed because I looked different and funny. Why was I so short? I wasn't that much shorter than some of them, but I looked different. On the playground, I never went on the teeter-totter. It was too high and scary. I couldn't get on it, and my feet didn't reach the ground. I was also scared to go on the swings because I wasn't tall enough to hop on or off. I would always miss the swing and end up falling down on my butt or, worse, hitting my head and scraping my hands and arms, which hurt a lot and I would cry. Some of the kids would see this and start laughing and showing off how they could swing high in the air.

Yeah, kindergarten—my beginning.

***

Around second grade I dared myself to give it another try, and I got on the swing and learned how to pump my legs and body back and forth to gain momentum and go higher. But I leaned too far back, lost my balance, and fell off the swing, hitting my head on the ground really hard. I couldn't move. It hurt so bad, and I was dizzy. I burst out crying. Although I was able to get up, my parents were called right away to take me home. My dad was afraid I had a concussion. Even though it turned out I didn't, I stayed home for a few days to rest and make sure I was okay. I was afraid I wouldn't be allowed to swing anymore because I had fallen off, but I needed and wanted to do it again, and I later would.

A Little Me

One thing I always appreciated about my parents was that they never panicked or overreacted. They never said I couldn't do anything. They didn't tell the school or the teachers I couldn't swing anymore. They never said it was too dangerous. If they weren't sure how I would manage something or were afraid for me, they never let on but would encourage me to try. They didn't want me to get the notion there were activities I couldn't do or dreams I couldn't achieve because I was different or because it would be too hard. And they definitely didn't want me to come up with excuses to get out of trying new things or doing things I needed to do. That would be taking the easy way out, using my dwarfism as an excuse.

My parents were not fans of making excuses. Nope, we were the Knight kids, and that meant we always needed to give it our best effort. No slacking. And if it didn't work out, it didn't work out. It wasn't going to be because I was different, a little person, or because others made fun of me or it was too hard. If I decided not to do something, it would be because it just didn't work out, my interests changed, or I grew out of it. They helped me learn how to get back up and try again. Okay, maybe I wouldn't be a professional basketball player even if I wanted to, but they always encouraged me to try, to dream big, and to believe I could do and be whatever I wanted. I might need to find different ways to accomplish my dreams, but my family had my back. They supported and encouraged me as best they could.

***

My early experiences in kindergarten—my challenges with the stool, being teased by the other kids, and playing on the playground—were the beginning of what I call the woodpecker effect in my life. I can't point to any one big event and say this changed my life. Instead, there were woodpecker moments here and there.

Woodpeckers are generally beneficial for a tree. They eat the insects that infest and can damage a tree. Occasionally though, woodpeckers will peck and peck and peck so many holes in a tree that they end up hurting it. Overall, they help the tree survive by getting rid of what is not good, but they may also kill the tree.

Rough times and challenges happen to everyone and can be healthy because these moments help us grow, develop resilience, and learn about ourselves and make us stronger. Or we can let these challenges defeat us. I sometimes let them defeat me.

I allowed the outside world to get to me, and the pecking no longer helped me but hurt me. It tore down a lot of what little self-confidence I had, lessened my self-image, and made me think I wasn't good enough. This was more influential than the positive affirmations that should have risen to the top. It wasn't one big incident but rather a lot of small ones—little negative pecks that built up throughout my life and combined to become a big thing in the long run.

I didn't often tell myself, *Yes, you are good enough, if not more than good enough, Amy.* As quickly as I believed the thought, I turned right around and tossed the positive attitude out the window the minute I stepped out the front door and encountered other people. It was crazy. I was on a merry-go-round and would sway one way, but didn't have enough courage to hang on to believing in myself. *Yes, Amy, you are great just the way you are.*

I started to think I was not going to have any friends. I wasn't like anyone else, and because I was different, why would anyone like me or want me as a friend? My thoughts went around and around in my head, but I kept them to myself and didn't tell my parents, my siblings, or even my closest friends until later in life. I kept a lot of my fears, thoughts, and dreams to myself.

As I grew up I began to think I needed to be more like everyone wanted me to be, to be like my average-size friends. I wanted to please everyone. It's not that I thought badly about myself, but I let my doubts and insecurities get in the way of thinking better of myself. Would whatever I did be good enough if I couldn't be like my average-size friends?

There was one significant moment in my life that did have an impact on me, and I reflected back on it to get me through college, in my married life, and still to this day. It's significant because it has reminded me over the years that when life gets tough, it's not the time to run away and give up, but to face it and forge ahead. When life seems difficult or a particular moment seems overwhelming, it's not the end of the world. You just pick yourself back up and try again, or start over in a new direction.

The first day of first grade arrived, and I refused to go. I had held on to some of my rough kindergarten moments and let them linger over the summer. I had gone shopping with my mom to get some new clothes, including a first-day-of-school outfit, and new school supplies that I couldn't wait to use. On one hand, I was definitely excited to start school, but on the other hand, I was scared to go. My parents said the typical things: it would be fun, there would be so many kids to make friends with, and I'd have so much fun learning and do so many activities that I wouldn't have time to think about anything else. Those encouraging thoughts were comforting for a little bit, but the feeling was fleeting.

Some of the thoughts that went through my young mind were, *How much taller will they be than me? Will I make friends? Will they like me? What can I do so they won't notice as much that I'm different from them? Will any of the kids play with me on the playground?* Of course, just being myself would have been the best remedy, but I didn't think that would be enough. So when the first day of school arrived, my thoughts overwhelmed me and I refused to go.

Getting ready on that first day of school was a little different in my family than for most families I knew at the time. My mom had decided she wanted to return to work and had gotten her first job since having kids. Her first day at her new job was also the first day of school. At that time a lot of women who still had young kids at home weren't looking for jobs or going to work. That movement was really just getting started then. My brother would be the first to have to go to preschool. A lot of changes seemed to be happening. My father had worked at his job as an architectural civil engineer at the Ford Motor Co. for only about five years.

My two older sisters were excited to head back to school and see their friends, wear their new first-day-of-school outfits, and find out what their friends had done over summer vacation. My sisters, six and four years older than me, were responsible for making sure I got ready on time and walking me to school. My mother took my brother to preschool, and my father left to go to work. Yet here I was, refusing to go no matter what my sisters told me or how much they pushed me. "Amy, you need to go to school. We're going to be late." "If you don't go, Mom and Dad are going to be so mad at you." "Come on, Amy, we want to go and see our friends. You're going to be fine," and so on. But I didn't budge. I started to cry. I didn't want anyone to be mad at me, and my sisters were, but I didn't want to face what I thought would happen at school.

I worked myself up into such a frenzy that I definitely made my first day of first grade so much worse than a first day of school should be. It should have been exciting and fun meeting new kids and making friends. I mean, it was first grade; it wasn't as if I were going away to college in a whole different state. Here I was, though, hiding in my room, crying and telling my sisters I wasn't going and they couldn't make me. They were beside themselves as to what to do with me. They couldn't leave me there alone while they went to school. Should they call Mom or Dad? Today was Mom's first day at her new job. They couldn't do that. And Dad? Well, they couldn't call him. They didn't know what to do, and now they would be late. Eventually, they ended up calling my dad and he came home to figure things out.

Looking back on how he handled the situation, that's how I hoped I would handle situations with my own kids: in a quiet, calm, yet firm way. I aspired to be like him. He didn't raise his voice; he didn't get angry at me and just force me to go. He wasn't passive and didn't give in to my tantrums. He showed me he cared by bending down and talking to me, letting me know he understood. I can remember crying and telling him I didn't want to go because I was too scared. "All of the kids are going to make fun of me because I'm not like them. I'm different. They're not going to want to be my friends."

My father sat down next to me and listened. He put his arm around me and, speaking in a way that comforted me, said, "You need to do things even if you don't want to, because it's the right thing to do. You'll be better off, and it'll all turn out better than you think, but you won't know if you don't go. Sure, there will be a few kids that won't want to be your friend. Yes, there will be a few kids that may make fun of you, but you don't have to be friends with them. Yes, you're shorter than they are, but if you don't go, you won't have the opportunity to choose whom you want to have as your friends, either."

He hoped I knew and remembered that he and my mom loved me very much and didn't want to see me upset or hurt. "But you need to go to school and let others get to know you, and then you can decide who your friends will be. Always know, Amy, that God doesn't make mistakes. You are exactly who you are supposed to be, and we are glad you are part of our family. Now, let's go show your class who Amy is."

I'm not sure what my father told his colleagues at work, but it wasn't typical for a man to take off work to handle a family issue at home. My dad did, though. He took my sisters and me to school and walked me to my class. Instead of walking into the classroom along with everyone else, there I stood, holding on to my dad's hand, and suddenly the kids turned around to look at me. The moment was long and uncomfortable. That's how I started first grade.

When I've experienced similar moments throughout my life—entering a room, beginning a new job, starting up a conversation with strangers—my thoughts go back to that moment in first grade when all I wanted to do was run away and hide from the situation. But I didn't. I pulled myself together and rose to the occasion and kept moving forward. I held my dad's hand and knew everything would be okay.

As I look back at this event in my life, it continues to remind me that God doesn't make mistakes. I matter, I'm worth it, and I have a purpose. That will never change. My first day of first grade was like a peck from a woodpecker that changed my life. It didn't destroy me, but it let me know life wasn't going to be easy, yet I don't have to make it so hard and run from it either. In fact, life can be darn right, wonderfully great.

Encouragement from Amy:

~Allow yourself to reflect on the past. Whether it was good or not, we'll always learn from our past, so we can be better in the present. But don't live there. If you do, you'll often miss opportunities in the present and think there is no future.

CHAPTER 3

Adapting to My World

A Little Me

Our character, a part of who we are, comes from our past, from the environment we grew up in—our family life, friends, school, childhood experiences, teenage years, and our arrival into adulthood. And the memories we hold on to from our growing-up days play a part in who we are and how we perceive life.

As we get older, the memories we cherish the most seem to linger and play a more significant part in our present and future. These are the memories we hope supersede the uglier, more uncomfortable ones, the ones that have a tendency to lurk in the corners of our minds. The memories and experiences we hold on to from the past, and how we perceive them, can be a big factor in moving forward into adult life. How much of our past we bring into our present and future does matter.

Of course I don't want to forget my past, but I probably should have let some of it go long before I did—the name-calling, the bullying, being made fun of, often being overlooked, being treated as a friend one moment but then being let go when someone "better" came along, and so much more. By hanging on to these experiences, I was shielding myself from future pain.

Letting go is brave. Not having to carry that baggage in my mind would have lightened my load. I'm glad I finally gained enough courage and strength to realize my past experiences are learning opportunities and don't have to be a burden.

Throughout my life I've had a tendency to hold back on expressing myself to my friends, family, and others. I wanted to be perfect, to make sure I said and did the right things all the time. I didn't want to say anything negative or express an opinion that people might disagree with, because I wanted others to like me and I didn't like confrontation. I feared saying or doing things that could give anyone one more excuse not to like me because I was different.

Regardless of who the other person was or whether I'd chosen to have a friendship with him or her, I just wanted to be liked. I was a people pleaser to the detriment of my own good. The problem was I worried more about what others thought and how they might perceive me than what I thought of myself. So I tried to craft what I said and talked about with others so my communication would be pleasing and perfect. What a daunting task I put on myself!

I found I could be so careful in what and how I said anything that I could keep others at a distance so I wouldn't get hurt, instead of just expressing my true thoughts and opinions. I've come a long way, and I'm glad I'm less of a people pleaser than I used to be, but it does still surface at times and catches me off guard when I find myself doing it. It's one thing to enjoy doing things for others, but it's another thing entirely when we do something simply to be liked. When we feel we have something to hide, something we don't want others to know because we're afraid of what they will think, well, that's not a good feeling to have or a way to live.

Over time I found myself not building up strong character traits like discernment, courage, strength, confidence, and purpose because I wanted to be liked, and I convinced myself there was nothing wrong with other people but there was something wrong with me. I know it wasn't healthy, but I got in this rut of thinking and stayed in it for a long time. Crazy, I know, but this kind of thinking began when I was young. I'm not sure how or why I had such low self-confidence. It didn't begin with my family life. What did come from my family was a foundation in faith and the belief that I'm good just the way I am.

A Little Me

The outward image I had came from perceptions of what I saw, felt, and experienced from others, books, movies, and media. Someone different was never the hero, and I certainly didn't have the beauty of an average-size woman, or so I thought. The perceptions I gathered and experienced crept into my mind-set ever so subtly. I've definitely had my physical challenges, but I think I created my emotional challenges myself.

I grew up in a good, loving, traditional family. My father was hardworking; he provided for his family and spent time with his children. I put my father on a pedestal. He was my hero. He was confident and the solver of problems. He fixed things and figured out ways I could adapt to obstacles in my life, such as altering my bike and my car pedals when I started to drive. He was firm yet soothing and didn't seem to get too shook up over life. Life was good and everything would work out when I was with my dad.

As a working mother, my mom showed me determination and how to follow a dream. She pursued a career and was still able to manage her family and household. She always suggested I get out there and try different things—church camp, gymnastics, art—and I did for a while. I learned to push myself sometimes, but other times I ended up retreating. Why? I don't know. What-ifs got in the way, and I just got scared. Scared of failure and of success at the same time. Despite being a working mother, my mom was a perfectionist when it came to keeping the house clean and keeping life orderly.

My parents had a good relationship; they loved each other and their children. I also saw that they weren't perfect. Although they argued a lot, they always seemed to work it out and stay true to each other and our family. In their relationship I saw that life isn't perfect; there will always be challenges but also a way to figure them out. You just need to do the best you can. The saying is, "If you don't try, then you have failed already." My parents have always given their marriage their all. *Failure* and *can't* weren't used in my family. If I said I couldn't do something, my father would say, "There is no such word as *can't* because there are always ways to figure it out."

I didn't grow up with a "lovey gushy" mom and dad. Yes, I knew they loved me, and they often told me how proud they were of all I had accomplished, but as I look back, I was probably looking for and needed a little more affirmation. I still don't understand why I had low self-esteem and confidence in myself. It was as though my mind couldn't reconcile what my parents told me with how I believed others thought of me. I had a positive outlook on life and held my own—at least, that was the outward image I projected—but I hid how scared I was of not meeting their expectations. I needed and wanted to hear more positive affirmations about how I was a good person, beautiful, and bright, and yes-you-can encouragement from my parents and friends than I got.

What I did know was that my parents always loved me and truly believed in me. I could do anything and be anything I put my mind to. I just had to convince myself to believe it.

I'm thankful my parents didn't cater to me growing up just because I was a little person and different from my siblings. They could have rearranged our family life, such as putting dishes in the lower cabinets in the kitchen. They could have lowered the sink in the bathroom so it would have been easier for me to use. They could have made the things I used most often, on an everyday basis, more convenient for me to reach, and I wouldn't have had to climb up and down and use stools all the time. They could have gone beyond our home and into my school to pave the way for me. They could have made all of those challenges go away so I didn't have to deal with them. They could have painted a picture of my life with no problems, where everything was taken care of and I didn't have to face all the things that came my way, because I was a little person, their precious daughter.

They didn't do any of those things. Instead, they encouraged me not to run from difficult situations. They helped me learn to adapt and, specifically, to use stools because they would always be a part of my everyday life. They helped me learn how to solve the problems I encountered without running to them to solve everything for me. When I needed help, advice, or support I knew they were always there, standing on the sidelines, ready to jump in.

What my parents gave me was an environment I could be comfortable in and where I felt safe to try different ways to accomplish everyday life and face my challenges. They gave me a family and a physical environment, a home, that told me I could. I could do it on my own, and I had the ability to do most anything. When I fell, physically or emotionally, they helped and taught me how to pick myself up.

If they had made it too easy for me at home, I wouldn't have wanted to leave and wouldn't have learned to figure out how to adapt. I learned how to do things my way. Otherwise, I might not have survived the "outside world" as well as I have. Once I walked out the front door each day, the world wouldn't always be easy and kind, but it wouldn't necessarily be horrible, mean, and hard either. It's a world to explore and grow in—embrace the adventure.

Growing up in my home, I learned the basics and developed a good foundation. I learned I am a part of life and other people's lives, and not separate from others just because I'm different. We all need to learn to adapt to something in our lives and face challenges in one way or another. I was not brought up to expect others to accommodate me just because I'm different, a little person. I wasn't brought up to expect others to readily jump to the occasion to assist me without my asking first. I can do for myself and ask for help when I can't.

I learned to climb on the kitchen stool and onto the kitchen counters to get a glass or anything else I needed in the cupboards. I needed a stool to reach the higher shelves in the refrigerator and pantry. I needed a stool in the bathroom and my bedroom closet. Stools were so much a part of my life that I didn't even think about them not being available everywhere until I went to school or got a job or went shopping.

I adapted at home, but the outside world was a whole different program. My home environment helped me gain the confidence I needed to see I could do a lot of things myself, like everyone else, just in a slightly different way. When I left each day for school it didn't seem as easy as it did at home, and I allowed that difference to trip me up a lot more than I should have. I felt that I looked awkward in how I did things, and I didn't like others to see that.

Although I didn't get teased all the time, every day, relentlessly, I was teased enough that it chipped away at my confidence and felt as if others thought there was something wrong with me. I didn't think there was anything wrong with me, though. My classmates would make fun of me for being so short and laugh when I couldn't reach things. They said I was like a baby and shouldn't be in first grade. Sometimes I found my stool gone or hidden in the classroom, which made me feel horrible because what I needed to be independent was gone.

Instead of asking for help, I preferred to do without. Even though deep down I felt good about myself as a person, that didn't always translate when I was outside of my home or away from my family. I wasn't used to asking anyone for help. I was used to telling myself I could do this on my own, if I had my stool. With it I could reach the higher bookshelves when I wanted to check out a book, I could wash my hands in the bathroom, I could do so much more with a lot more ease instead of having to ask for someone's help.

Throughout my school years I began to learn that the world isn't here to adapt to me because I'm different, but rather that I need to adapt to the world in a way that helps me accomplish what I want to do and be what I want to be. If I couldn't do something myself, I had better learn to ask for help. I was a little stubborn sometimes and tried to be independent, so it took quite a while for me to feel comfortable asking for help. If I asked for help to do something that most anyone could do, I felt inadequate and it reminded me yet again that I was different.

It wasn't as if I didn't know I was different; I just didn't like to constantly be reminded of it, especially when I was with others. Later in life I finally realized I wasn't allowing people to get to know me because the big elephant in the room got in my way. And the big elephant was, I was a little person. A dwarf. I forgot to remind myself, *I am still Amy.* I let the teasing from the other kids get to me, and looked at it as a negative thing instead of turning it around into something positive. I knew I was good enough, but thoughts of inadequacy still took hold.

What my father told me back in first grade kept me moving forward and reminded me to think more positively about myself. I hang on to those words every day. My faith was and is my foundation. I love going to church, learning and hearing God's word. These words remind me that God is big. He is bigger than me, bigger than any challenge, and bigger than anyone else. He doesn't make mistakes. So if others thought I wasn't good enough or if I thought I wasn't good enough, well, I was good enough for him and nothing could top that.

The old saying "Sticks and stones will break my bones, but words will never hurt me" was something I heard a lot, but over the years, I've come to realize how impactful and hurtful words can be. I've never wanted people to gush over me and tell me how great I am just for the sake of saying it. I'd rather they speak with honesty and sincerity. I took a lot of things too seriously. I needed to lighten up. Constructive criticism is meant for good. The hard part is knowing good intentions from harmful ones.

Once in a while it is nice when someone does or says something kind just because they know you need it. I was brought up to do and say nice things to encourage others. I was also brought up to give and give when someone is in need, but not to give with the expectation of getting something in return or because it brings attention back to myself. If we do that, what is the value in giving?

Why not begin every day by giving positive affirmations to ourselves? When we find something good and say something positive, it's amazing what an impact that can have on our attitude and perspective throughout the whole day.

I was teased a lot in grade school and on the playground. Later, in junior high and high school, I was ignored and didn't feel included. I was shy, and it was hard for me to put myself out there. I was good enough to hang out in a group, but wasn't invited to parties or included in other outings. I learned to hide my feelings and fears because I didn't want others to know how afraid and hurt I felt. I put on a good front a lot of the time and pretended it was no big deal.

Walking home from school one day in third grade, after staying late to finish up a project with my teacher, I encountered an older boy, a fifth- or sixth-grader, walking on the other side of the street, who seemed to be following me. I didn't recognize him, so I started to walk faster. I felt scared because I was alone. He kept following me and then began to yell and call me names and say crude things to me. "You're nothing because you're so short. Why are you so small? Look at you; you're so funny and ugly looking you must be a mistake. How can anyone like you? You shouldn't be here." I was very scared and intimidated, and started to cry. If I could only make it home, then everything would be okay.

Because my mom worked every day, we had a housekeeper/babysitter so we could go home after school. I tried to get away from this boy who was teasing me by hurrying as fast as I could to get to home. I was so glad when I finally saw my house. By this time, he had stopped yelling and calling me names. I'm not sure if he knew where I lived, but I was just so glad it had stopped. When I came to my house and walked up the driveway to the back door, he kept walking past my house, on the other side of the street.

I didn't say anything to our housekeeper or my siblings, and I didn't say anything to either of my parents when they got home. I didn't think I needed to bother them. I didn't want them to know what this boy had done or what the other kids were saying to me. I felt like I needed to handle it all by myself, to prove to myself it would all be okay, given enough time. Why make a big deal over something that others might think was really no big deal? I was afraid to go back to school because I didn't know this boy, if he went to the same school I did, or if this would happen to me again and again. I didn't know what he might have told his friends or what the other kids might have heard.

I kept my feelings and fears to myself. I tried to be strong by pretending it didn't bother me. On the outside it was, *Don't let them see you're scared.* But on the inside I just wanted to run away from it all.

I often felt scared and alone. I realized being different does make some people scared of you, meaning kids were scared of me. I didn't want others to be afraid of me. That didn't make me feel good at all. I saw that some people hurt others with words just to feel better about themselves, but that wasn't a good-enough reason for why anyone would want to scare me, tease me, call me names, and make me feel lessened.

"Sticks and stones will break my bones, but words will never hurt me" is so not reality. Words do hurt, and they hurt beyond the surface. They go deep to the heart and core of people sometimes. I let words erode my confidence and make me feel less than and not good enough. I couldn't hide or change myself physically, but I did have the ability to change my attitude and outlook. I just didn't have the tools then to know how to do that.

I chose not to say anything to anyone about what was happening to me at and after school. I really don't know why, but something held me back. It wasn't that I couldn't talk to my parents. For some reason, I felt like I had to figure it out on my own

In junior high I still wasn't on the school bus route, so I had to walk a mile to and from school each day. Since I could physically walk the distance—sure, it may have taken me a little longer than my average-size friends, but I could do it—I didn't think to ask my parents to advocate with the school for me to be allowed to walk just a few blocks to ride the bus to school, and since I didn't complain, they didn't think to ask about it either. In the winter I really wished I had pushed to ride the bus because it was tough to walk to school in the deep snow.

An older boy had been taunting me on and off for months. This hadn't happened since grade school. I had hoped I wouldn't have to endure this again. This time I mentioned it to my brother, who, even though he was younger than me, always felt the need to protect and watch over me. He told me, if this happened again, to let him know and he'd deal with the kid so he wouldn't bother me anymore.

Walking home late after band practice one day, this boy once again began following and taunting me. As his language got rougher, cruder, meaner, and sexual in nature, I panicked that this would be the time I got hurt. I couldn't ignore what was happening to me so often anymore. I didn't know anyone who lived in the houses I passed to get home to ask for help. I didn't know this boy either. I didn't know what to do and was tired of feeling scared walking home from school.

Third grade came flashing back to me, as did a memory of a fight I had with a boy on the playground in fourth grade, who had teased me until I finally retaliated in kind. He was shorter than the other boys, so I thought just maybe he faced things similar to what I did. He was a boy who didn't quite fit in with the other boys. Why he picked on me and got in a fight with me, I really don't know. Neither of us ended up winning, and the other boys teased him for fighting a girl. But I felt pretty proud for sticking up for myself for once. I always wondered if he hurt like I did.

As I walked home with this bigger, older boy taunting me, again all I could think about was getting home safely. I kept thinking, *Just stay focused and don't respond or look at him. Don't give him the time of day or let him think what he's doing is getting to you.* He kept following me and saying mean and awful things at me.

I finally got to my street and saw that my brother was home. Turning into my driveway, I turned around and yelled at him to leave me alone and go away. I waited by the back door to see if he would walk on past my house. I couldn't believe it when he followed me into my driveway. Terrified, I ran in the house and told my brother. He barely listened to all I had to tell him before going outside. He was mad, very mad, and was not going to let this boy get away with what he was doing to me.

The boy was standing in the driveway, taunting my brother, saying, "What are you going to do about it?" Why, oh why, was this happening to me? Even though my brother was tall and physically fit for his age, he was also about four years younger, and this boy was bigger. I didn't want my brother to get hurt. I didn't want him to fight this boy. My heart was beating so fast.

They started to fight, punching each other in our driveway. Crying and scared, I yelled for them to stop. Finally, the boy got up from the ground after my brother punched him, and ran off down the street. It was over, or so I hoped. Maybe this would be the last time I ever saw this boy. My brother had a bloody nose and was hurting, but he was okay. Afterward, whenever I walked home from school, I kept looking over my shoulder to see if anyone was following me, but no one ever was. I never was bothered by or saw that boy again. But for months I didn't feel safe walking home by myself after school.

A Little Me

All of this on-again, off-again harassment was from what? Because I was different? I just didn't understand why. I'm sure a lot of my lack of self-confidence stems from experiences I had growing up. Sometimes it's still hard to fight hanging on to it, and other times I feel invincible. Through it all I've remained strong because of my faith. It's the one thing I've always hung on to. At the time I didn't understand why all of this was happening just because others saw me as different. Was it really all about them wanting to feel better about themselves? I just didn't get it. I was confused.

I always felt horrible after doing something I knew wasn't right, or if I knew I had hurt someone. That horrible feeling I got often stopped me ahead of time, as I'd rather avoid the guilt that inevitably followed. That's probably why I don't like confrontation. I didn't learn how to communicate disagreements or differences in opinion well. Communication is a powerful tool and worth knowing how to apply to different situations. Did I scare people that much, or was I so different that people had to react to me in a negative way?

I had a few good friends, but I always worried some stranger or someone I didn't know well would call me crude or mean names in public. I felt so small when that happened and worried my friends would suddenly think differently of me. They didn't, though. They backed me up. As my father told me years ago, I get to decide who my friends are, and I think I have learned well over the years to choose my friends and the community of people I want to have around me, and to be a friend to others.

I recently asked a longtime friend of mine what she remembered about our childhood. She told me she didn't like it when she saw the kids staring at me in line after the bell rang during recess, teasing, and whispering about me behind my back. I didn't hear what they were saying, but I felt it. She heard it, though. It became a part of my life, the snickering, the staring and pointing at me in public. I began to try to ignore it; I didn't want to hear it anymore. Maybe no one really saw or heard it but me. I hoped when my friends did, they wouldn't decide to walk out of my life or look at me differently, but would still just see me as Amy, their friend who just happened to be different. Being with someone who is different, who is being stared at or made fun of, can change not only your perspective of yourself but also of your friend. I always hoped my friends didn't feel uncomfortable being with me.

As much as we want to ignore our differences and see ourselves as all the same or just like someone else, we aren't. I truly believe that once we do that, we stop appreciating our differences and what makes each of us unique. Once we recognize that we are all different, we can move on and begin to appreciate our similarities. And our similarities can help us better understand and appreciate each other. Focusing on our differences can drive us apart, but our similarities can bring us together. We are not the same, we are different. We all want to be a part of something; to be liked; to feel included, appreciated, loved, valued, that we matter, and are more than good enough; to be successful; to have friendships, opportunities, and others to help us; and so much more. As we hope for these things in our lives, we need to understand that others do too.

Over time I've come to appreciate that it's okay to be different. Not everyone is going to like me or embrace my difference, and that's okay too. I'm not always going to do a good job no matter how hard I try, but I know I'll always do my best, given the opportunity. It's okay to change your mind and go in another direction. It's okay to ask for help. It's not only okay but it's healthy. It's important to learn to like yourself. Our similarities can be the bridge that brings us together.

I can't imagine living my life without my Christian faith. It has always been a big part of my life. I'm never alone because God is always with me. We are not born with resilience. Resilience is a muscle that needs to be developed, and one way it's strengthened is through the challenges we face. I've not always faced my challenges in the most constructive way, but because of my faith, I've faced them instead of running away, and as a result, I overcame them.

My strength comes through being resilient—steady as she goes. When I was younger, I didn't have a lot of resilience. I survived, but I was slow at learning how to thrive. There were many, many times I wanted to give up and check out on life. A few times it scared me. I cried a lot when I was alone in my bedroom because I felt lonely and lost, and thought maybe it would be easier to not be here anymore. But I didn't want to disappoint my parents, to run away instead of dealing with what was going on and letting someone know what I was going through. And I was a little bit curious to see how my life turned out.

What my father told me as a young girl, "God doesn't make mistakes," anchored me enough to keep going. I didn't have the right to check out on life, to give up because I didn't feel as though I could handle it anymore. It felt cheap and easy, and I didn't want to be like that. My faith truly was my saving grace. I had dreams and goals, and I wanted to see if I could make them come true. *Life* is a reason to get up the next day, go after it, and not give up. God will not give up on me, so I shouldn't either.

Amy Roloff

I'm better at letting the uncomfortable, challenging, embarrassing times slide off my shoulders and out of my thoughts, and not taking things so seriously or placing such importance on what may be said or done. I'm thankful that the older I get the wiser I am, and I focus more on what I can do and how I react instead of what I can't control—other people's opinions or thoughts about me, and their actions.

Encouragement from Amy:

~I can't control what anyone does or thinks about me. What I can control is what I think about myself and how I handle and react to situations and the people around me. What we do and say does impact our lives and others around us as well.

CHAPTER 4

Others like Me

Life is full of opportunities and challenges, successes and failures. I admit, I haven't always done the best job of overcoming some of my challenges, and I've missed opportunities, but in the end, I am who I am because of them and the choices I've made. Some lessons I've learned in my life are to continuingly believe in myself, that my attitude is crucial, to pick myself up when I fall, to do the best I can, and to own the choices I've made. Life is a journey, and it's not always pretty, but there is a whole lot of life to live, more good than not.

Over time I've realized my attitude has played, and still does play, a *big* part in my life. Just as it does for all of us. We hear over and over again that having a positive attitude is important for our success. We may hear this so often that it loses its importance and we forget that what we think and say does matter. Our attitude makes a difference in how we live, look at things, face challenges, and embrace our successes. We can choose to see our lives as hard or challenging, or in all sorts of negative ways. Our thoughts may be, *Why me? I can't. It's not fair.* Or we can choose to see our challenges with a more positive mind-set, viewing them as learning and growing opportunities or new possibilities. My attitude affects how I think of myself right now. *Am I worthy? Do I matter? Am I important? Am I beautiful? Do I deserve a chance? Am I a success or a failure?*

How much baggage I bring from my past into my present will affect my future. I can choose whether my past is a hindrance or a benefit.

We shouldn't try to forget or erase our past, because it's a part of us, our character, but neither should we dwell on it and waste valuable time and resources that could be invested into the present and future. We can't go back and change it even if we wanted to. We need to acknowledge the past and realize it can still have a negative impact on us. But our past can also have a positive impact and be the stepping stone that launches us right where we want to be. The past helps shape us and plays a part in how we decide to live today and in the future.

I don't agree with dismissing another's challenge as insignificant, with a "get over it" attitude, just because we may not think it's a big deal. What may seem small to us may be big to him or her. Until we walk in someone else's shoes, we can't assume he or she should have acted, said, or done something differently, but we can have empathy and offer support and encouragement.

Everyone wants to feel loved, accepted, and appreciated, and to know someone cares. I appreciate when people respond honestly and sincerely to me when I reach out to them, instead of patronizing me. I'm not perfect and would rather have people think highly enough of me to give me their honest input instead of inflating my ego and telling me what they think I want to hear. It's important to have a good, strong personal community around yourself that is positive, constructive, supportive, encouraging, honest, and one that you want to be a part of, to give of yourself and receive from one another. It doesn't have to be a large number of individuals, but rather individuals you trust and care about.

I've often built up a protective wall around myself so I didn't have to let anyone in and risk pain and rejection. In turn, I made it harder for others to be supportive and encouraging, and get to know me. My attitude came across as, "I can do it all by myself. I don't need anyone," yet I wanted friends. I couldn't have it both ways, though. If I needed help, then the spotlight would show me as incapable and different, or so I thought. It's hard to be vulnerable, and I preferred to let others take that risk first instead of me; it was easier. This way,

A Little Me

I still felt like I was projecting this persona of being a little-person woman with no problems—*my life is great, I can do anything just like anyone else, I can't get hurt.* Why give anyone a reason to think I was less than them? I wanted to appear positive and strong, as if I could handle anything even though I didn't feel like it on the inside.

Any true friendship or relationship can't be a one-way street. Both people need to be invested. I played these mental games because I didn't want others to see the real me. I didn't think they would like it. The wall I built up was meant to have others see what I wanted them to see. If I let them in, well, I might not be good enough anymore. I wouldn't take even the slightest chance of hearing that.

Growing up, most of my experiences were not sad and horrible. My family and friends weren't insensitive and uncaring. In fact, I had a wonderful childhood filled with a lot of fond memories. I just got stuck for many years focusing on my outside package—being a dwarf—and didn't pay enough attention to the inside package. The perception we have of ourselves does have an impact on our lives and affects us in many different ways. How I saw myself, how I thought others saw me, and how others really looked at me never seemed to match up. Those perceptions were unbalanced, and I think I caused a lot of that unbalance myself.

My late-elementary and early-high-school years were tough on me. But I won't blame the mistakes I've made on the challenges I've had in life or play "poor me" because life was tough and I'm a dwarf. If I did, then I would have to ignore the beauty and success I had in those years as well. I think we can learn a lot from others when we know a little of their past and see how they got to where they are now. We all have to face something in our lives, and how we have dealt with it has helped us to survive and get where we are now. The question is, do we want to just survive, or would we rather thrive? You can't thrive if you keep living in the past.

I can't erase my past regardless of how I remember or view it now, and I don't want to. It's a part of me. But I shouldn't dwell on it either. Though sometimes, as situations arise, my past comes crashing in on me. Sometimes those memories are sad, negative, or difficult, and other times they are of proud accomplishments, great times, or success, and are loving, happy, and meaningful because those experiences made me a better person. I lived my life the best way I knew how despite this thing called dwarfism. I'm just Amy.

I always go back to that first day in first grade and what my father said, "God doesn't make mistakes," when I'm feeling off and depressed or stuck. It brings me back to reality and reminds me that I can't let so many of those moments in my life be more than what they should be: the past. Besides, there are too many wonderful, spectacular moments to remember instead.

I'm often asked if I have ever wished I were average height, and to be frank, the answer is no. I never wished I were average height, but what I did wish sometimes, probably more often than I care to remember, was that my life would be like an average-size person's life. What I saw as an average-height life just seemed less challenging with so many more opportunities than mine did, being a dwarf. How could I have that kind of life being me, a little-person woman?

That's just it: I focused so much on what I was and what I was not that I didn't pay enough attention to *who* I was and what I wanted to do. I was capable of more. I am a woman who has goals, dreams, hopes, fears, happiness, laughter, love, and a whole lot to offer and a life to live.

A Little Me

Growing up, my family took an annual two-week vacation, usually camping. I loved the outdoors: campfires, hiking, canoeing, fishing, and just being in nature and seeing the beautiful outdoors all around me. Camping reminded me that simple things are great too. Seeing nature all around me was inspiring. Everyone should get away and experience it, leave *life* behind for a moment to fully embrace the natural world. It will inspire you and help you appreciate your life. You gain a different perspective and outlook so when you return to reality you're ready to get back to it and live it. It does for me anyway.

My family camping trips reminded me to let go in order to embrace what was right in front of me. Let the past go. Allow new things and experiences to come into your life, and appreciate it when they do.

I have this simple place I like going back to in my home state of Michigan, up north at my parents' cabin on Lake Michigan. Over the years, it's been this peaceful yet powerful place I have gone to reflect on a lot of things in my life—my hopes, my fears, my dreams, and sometimes my crazy ideas and plans that seem impossible, but when I'm there they always seem possible. Just sitting on the beach with a campfire, hearing the waves crash upon the shore, seeing the sun sink into the distant horizon, and watching the beautiful stars come out at night is so amazing. I know this incredible, beautiful creation is God's way of inspiring me to give all of my worries to him. Being alone and appreciating what is around me helps me stop comparing myself to others, at least for the moment.

My life is full of so much more than I could have imagined. I can do anything I put my mind and talents to. And when I leave to go back home, everything looks brand-new again, full of hope and excitement. The back corner of our farm, overlooking the rolling farmland, trees, the little country church, and the coastal mountain range in the distance, where we have had so many campfires, is also one of my happy places that inspire me.

On one of our family camping trips, my parents and I met a family with a son who was also a little person. I didn't really think anything of it since I was ten years old and he was older than me. During this casual encounter, they told us about an organization called Little People of America (LPA)—a nonprofit organization for those four feet ten and under due to a medical condition. My parents had never heard of it before but took the information and made a point to find out more about it. They felt it was important that I know there were other people around with dwarfism just like me.

When I went to my first LPA chapter event held in my local area, I was so nervous. What would it be like to see others like me? Would I fit in? Would they like me? Would I look like them? The event was held at a roller-skating rink, and I was glad I already knew how to roller skate. I skated often with a few friends on our street and had gone skating for my birthday one year. At least that wouldn't be new.

As I entered the rink with my parents, I suddenly saw so many little people. You would think I would have been excited and happy to see others who looked a lot like me. I wasn't, though. I looked at everyone and wanted to run right out the door and go home. I started to cry, I was so scared. When I looked at everyone else I didn't see myself at all. No way did I look like them. This was not what I saw when I looked in the mirror every morning. My world was the average-size world, not this one. Not this small gathering of little people having a great time with each other. I saw little people who came in all different shapes and sizes and physical abilities, just like everyone else, yet I felt different and didn't feel like I belonged, at least not right away.

A Little Me

As any good parent would do, my dad took my hand and took me aside to tell me it would be okay and to try to have a good time. "Go out there and meet some of them. You never know what friends you'll make until you meet them. You need to give others a chance to get to know you as well, Amy." I wiped my tears away and said okay, but I told him not to go anywhere and to watch me just in case. What "just in case" meant was I wanted to make sure I still had a way out in case things didn't turn out well. I wanted to have an escape route, to be able to run out the door, get in the car, and go home. I was doing exactly what I didn't want others to do to me, making a quick judgment about other people just because they looked different.

I had put on my roller skates and started out onto the rink when a few of the other attendees came up to me and asked me to skate with them. Of course I felt pretty good then, but also a little hesitant. This was so new to me, being around others who looked like me. It was as though I was seeing a little of myself for the very first time, because I saw a part of me in them. Everyone seemed comfortable and happy, and they were genuinely friendly and full of life. Yeah, they might have looked a little funny, but their attitude toward life and other people was positive. They didn't seem to care what anyone else thought about them. So we went out on the roller-skating rink and started to skate. I saw other people looking at all of us and pointing fingers, but it didn't bother me as much as it would have if I had been by myself. I guess being with others does give you strength. Hopefully, I could take that strength away with me when I left.

One of the games being played was a skating race, and I thought for sure I could do this, and after seeing everyone in our group, I thought I could win. As we lined up, I thought, *No problem, I've got this in the bag.*

The race began, and as we skated, people left the rink until there were just a few of us left still skating. I was way ahead of the other racers, so I slowed up—I didn't want to blow everyone away—and kept looking behind me to see where the other skaters were. We were on the last round when suddenly a little-person woman, a little older than me, skated right past me and won. I couldn't believe it. I was shocked and, frankly, a little embarrassed. I could have and should have won, but I didn't because I let up. I suddenly had an ego. I heard my father's voice: "Never give up in anything in life until you cross the finish line or the whistle blows." I wanted a do-over. It was a reminder to me to always do my best.

That moment became one of many life lessons I hope I don't forget. Never assume you are better or less than anyone else, and don't count your chickens before they are hatched. I let up because, why give it my all if I had already won? I let up because of pride. I was going to show them how physically able I was. Even if you see the finish line, don't give up until you cross it. You need to give your best all the way through, not just in the beginning, halfway through, or toward the end, because having to play catch-up is not easy to do. To give and be your best is to do your best all the time, not just sometimes or when you feel like it. And you shouldn't only give your best when you think it matters or when others are paying attention, but in everything you do in life—socially, personally, physically, and professionally. That's how I was taught. It wasn't always easy, but it's what brought me back to, *Get off your duff, pick yourself up, and dust yourself off.*

It reminds me of the fable about the tortoise and the hare. The hare was fast and definitely could have beaten the tortoise, but he got distracted and too full of himself. The tortoise was slow but steady and focused. The fable ends with the tortoise passing the hare and winning the race. The hare couldn't believe it. Never give up.

That first LPA chapter event in my home area taught me a lot about myself and about a community that gave more to me than I ever expected it would. It all started from a chance encounter during a family camping trip and a roller-skating event. We all are different, have different talents and capabilities, and are beautiful and wonderful just the way we are. In that moment, I realized a little bit more that if I wanted others to see the good, the beauty, and the wonderfulness in me, then I needed to see those things in them as well.

Over the years, I've learned a lot from the many awesome little people I've met about life, perseverance, tenacity, determination, being comfortable with who I am, and the enjoyment of living life regardless of my physical limitations and being different. By attending that first event, I became a part of an organization where I felt like I belonged and where many little people changed the world for other little people. They accomplished more than I thought possible because they believed they could, they fought for their success; it was important, and it was worth the time and sacrifice they made. Over the course of my life, they have inspired me to try to reach beyond what I thought I could do. Sometimes I did go above and beyond, and other times I didn't, but I had role models I could look up to who reminded me, yes, I can. It is possible.

I left this Little People event feeling so glad my parents had taken me. I hoped we would go back again and again because I wanted to meet as many other little people my age as I could. I wanted to have friends who looked like me, that I could talk to face-to-face. But most importantly, I simply wanted friendship. There was so much to share, and we got it—I could better relate to them, and they could relate to me. There was a camaraderie with them that I didn't quite have with my other friends, and it felt good.

Looking back, I wish I had attended more LPA events in my growing-up years. I think it would have provided a bridge in those years that would have helped my self-confidence, sense of identity, and acceptance and appreciation of who I was. My parents assumed I would have asked them to take me more often if I had wanted to go, but I didn't nag them because I think I wanted them to push me a little harder and convince me to go. When I was older and in college I did decide to go more on my own. It felt like the perfect time to get out there more and get to know other little people, to learn from their experiences, embrace our commonality, enjoy doing things together, and make lifelong memories and friendships.

However, I knew the little-people world was not my world. It complemented my life, and it was a part of my life, but it was not "my life." I did so much outside of that community, just because that seemed to be the way it was, that it felt a little foreign when I did attend events and conferences with other little people. Yet I still needed to learn how to be more comfortable and confident being the only one different in the average-size world around me. It took me a long time. I still wanted to be liked and have the life an average-size person seemed to have, one that was less challenging and more successful.

How wrong I was.

Whatever package you come in, life isn't easier or harder than another's because you are different physically. There may be more challenges, but still, everyone has challenges.

A Little Me

My wanting what an average-height person had is like the little white picket fence. So many of us look at others and want to be like them and have what they have. Envy, or covetousness, is not something you want to have creep into your mind. We strive to be more like someone else or to have what others have so much that we lose focus on being grateful for what we already have, who we are, and what our purpose is. Looking at others, we may think they have easier, more successful lives without pain, challenges, and failures. From the outside, they may appear to be getting from A to Z quicker and easier, but we fail to see what they may have had to face and overcome between A and Z to get where they are now. So of course their lives look easier and more desirable.

When we look on the other side of the little white picket fence, it usually does look a whole lot greener. Well, of course it would. They took the time to water their side. If we took more time to look on our own side of the fence and care for it, maybe our side would be just as green or greener, instead of brown and dying. It takes work, desire, determination, time, and passion to have the success you want to have.

Wanting the life I perceived an average-size person had, but not wanting to be average height, took a big toll on my mind-set growing up. I was ashamed and couldn't change who I was. There it is again, what my dad told me: God doesn't make mistakes. I am who I am. I didn't learn how to like and be comfortable with myself for a long time. To be happy with who we are and to do our best, we have to like ourselves first. I needed to forget about what was on the other side of the white picket fence and learn to like my side and to water it. When we like ourselves, a lot of self-doubt goes away and we can make a difference in someone else's life instead of focusing so much on ourselves.

I tried so hard to be liked by others, to fit in, and to be a part of the average-size world around me. Over time I created a disconnect between myself and life around me. I'm in the average-size world, but I'm not. I'm in the little-people world, but I didn't feel like I was. I'm able-bodied, but I can't do everything like everyone else. Because I had one foot in the average-size world, one foot in the little-people world, and a hand in the disabled world—yes, many do consider me disabled—I ended up putting myself in neutral because I didn't know what to think and it felt as if I didn't fit in anywhere. I did that to myself—no one else did but me.

Although gym class was a whole lot of fun because I love to compete and play games, I didn't always like gym class in school. Of course I loved playing with my friends on the playground, playing games and doing physical things. What I didn't like were the many activities I couldn't do or couldn't do as well as others. For example, I always wanted to climb the rope and make it to the top—you know, that long rope hanging from the ceiling that we all stood in line to take turns finding out how far up each of us could climb. It was hard, and I just didn't have the strength. When we played dodgeball I always got out early because the ball was thrown so hard that I couldn't catch it or I couldn't get out of the way quick enough.

In sixth grade, we had a physical activity day where a lot of games were set up and we were to try to do them all. For each one, a ribbon was given to the first-, second-, and third-place winners. One of the activities was a basketball throw. I wasn't thrilled about this one because I knew I wouldn't do well at it since everyone was taller than I was. The basketball net looked so high to me, and to get the ball in the net would be close to impossible. Of course, we had to at least make the effort to try each activity. I remember my dad saying, "If you don't make the effort, how do you know you can't do it and that it won't work out? Just do the best you can." Then I remembered the skating race, when I thought I had already won and so I didn't give it my all to the very end.

My turn came to step up to the free-throw line and try to throw as many balls into the net as possible in the allotted time. I didn't throw the ball using two hands over my head; I threw the ball underhand because I had more power and it was easier for me that way. To my surprise, the first ball went in. Then the second ball went in. I began to get the hang of it. The third time I threw the ball it went in. I couldn't believe it! I hadn't thought the first one would go in. I threw the fourth toss, and the ball went in again. I kept throwing until I missed, and then, with more time left, I kept going.

I made twelve baskets in a row and fourteen baskets total. Some of the girls around me were so surprised, but everyone gave me high fives. I had made the most baskets out of anyone so far. I was afraid to get too excited because surely someone would beat me since everyone was taller than I was. So I nervously waited on the sidelines, watching the other kids take their turns, hoping no one would beat me.

The next person only made eight baskets, the person after that made eleven, and after everyone finished taking their turns, no one made more baskets than I had. I won! Little me made the most baskets out of all of my taller, average-size classmates! I was so excited. It was my first first-place ribbon. I was so proud and happy. I did it, I actually did it! I couldn't wait to get home to tell my family. I got first place in the basketball toss.

Amy Roloff

It may seem like a small accomplishment now, but it felt like a big accomplishment to me at the time. It reminded me once again that I always need to give my best effort to whatever I try. If it works out, wonderful, and if it doesn't, try again. Otherwise, why expect that you'll have success if you give less than a hundred percent or quit too early? If we don't expect to succeed, most likely we won't. If we expect the minimum, then most likely we will get the minimum, nothing more. That moment showed me I needed to expect more from myself because I can. That moment showed me not to expect any less just because I'm a little person. Whatever happens, it won't be because I'm a little person, but because I gave up too quickly before really making the effort. Just as life will keep pecking and creating challenges, life will also give me moments when I can choose to see challenges as opportunities to succeed no matter the outcome.

I've had to look to my past many times to remind myself that I need to push myself in the present and be hopeful for the future; to not make the same mistakes, but to learn from them so I don't make them again. I look at my past to remind me that there were not only failures but a lot of successes as well. It wasn't always a hurtful, devastating time; there many more good and happy times.

Sometimes all it takes is a moment, a thought, or a role model to change your life; a family member, a friend, or an acquaintance to say, "Yes, you can, so take a risk and find out what you're made of." As I look back, I had many individuals and experiences that helped me be able to live my life as I have. My role models were my parents, several individuals in the little-people community, my kids, and my faith.

Encouragement from Amy:

~It is better to try and fail than not to try at all. Failure isn't bad; instead, it's a learning opportunity. Success isn't an end-all. When you do achieve success, that's not the time to quit, but to appreciate it and keep going.

CHAPTER 5

My Self-Image

Comparing ourselves to other people is something we women do way too often and take way too seriously. I have done it most of my life even though it was impossible for me to look or be like the women I saw in magazines and ads, or those who were the heroines in books.

Often we are persuaded by advertising from the fashion and cosmetics industries that we need this or that to feel and be beautiful. And we buy into this message. It's easy to do. However, most fashions don't fit or look good on my short body type because of my being a little person. As for cosmetics, I was convinced that no amount of makeup was going to make me look beautiful, yet I have lots of makeup in a drawer. I've compared myself to others in subtle ways all of my life, perhaps more in my younger years.

Now that I'm older I don't compare myself to images I see or place as much emphasis on my looks as I did when I was younger. But being divorced has made me realize I'm back on the road again of comparing myself to others. I don't want to go back to seeking approval from others again. I know I don't look like other women my age, and I shouldn't. After divorcing at my age I needed to re-learn to like myself and know I'm beautiful just as I am right now. I'm thankful I've learned to let go and not worry about my looks so much. I can't change my physical appearance, but I can change my attitude about it.

When you think you're the only one like yourself, it's easy to fall into thinking you're not good enough and start comparing yourself to others, which becomes an endless mind game that fools with your mind-set. I knew I had an unrealistic perception of myself; I knew I was better than I gave myself credit. Why on earth would I expect to look like someone else? Because I let magazines, ads, and TV tell me I needed to. For someone who only wanted to fit in and look like others, *pretty* didn't seem to be a word that fit me well, so why did I think I had to fit in with others?

As I look back, I'm a little disappointed at how much time and emphasis I placed on what I looked like, comparing myself to others, and the importance I gave to looks. I saw it all the time. What young girl growing up and trying to figure out who she is and how she fits in doesn't compare herself to others or some image she has in her mind of what she should look like? I wondered if I'd ever experience some of life's milestones, such as dating, career opportunities, marriage, and motherhood. Why I put so much importance on beauty, as if it were key to if I would date, have a career, get married, or have kids, is ridiculous now. So many of us women and girls still place too much emphasis on beauty, but I'm thrilled that this is getting better and we don't as much as we used to.

I recently went shopping for some baby clothes for my first grandchild—a grandson—and was reminded of how girls, from an early age, are bombarded with messages of how they should look. The clothing department was about three-quarters geared toward girls. I know, women shop and buy more than men, so of course it makes business sense. But so much importance is placed on a girl's beauty, and it speaks volumes to our self-image, more than we may realize. And since fashion changes all the time, it's hard to keep up. No wonder we are confused. This style was okay then but not now. That style is okay now but won't be next year. Going shopping for my first grandchild reminded me of how much I tried to fit into the fashion of the day and wore makeup to make me look pretty. Looking at baby clothes, I thought, *This is where it begins.*

A Little Me

In my day, bell-bottoms were the "in" fashion, and I so wanted to wear them. However, by the time I altered the pants, they were just like a regular pair of jeans because I had to cut the "bell" part off for the length to fit me. This was a big deal to a young girl like me, not being able to wear a certain style of fashion. It was another reminder that put me on the outside of the in crowd. A lot of what I wore needed alterations, but not everything I wore got altered. It would have been too expensive and taken too much time to have had all my clothes altered. Instead, I would just roll up my sleeves and make it work.

I've never thought it was a bad thing to want to look and feel good in what I wear and about my appearance, but when it became a determining factor to my self-worth, then it became a whole other thing. I wish I had expressed how I felt more often to my parents; maybe then I would have given them the chance to understand what I was going through and they could've helped me. I didn't, though. I wanted to show them, and myself, that I was confident, strong, and brave, and worrying about what I wore and looked like didn't feel strong, confident, and brave. The problem was basing my value—more or less, positive or negative—on fashion and cosmetics.

Fashion is a multimillion-dollar industry based on making people think they will look and feel better by wearing its products, but it should definitely not be a measure of our value. Obsessing over our outsides takes up our time when we should be working on our insides—our character. Fashion and cosmetics help us feel like somebody, but we forget we already *are* somebody. I thought if I could improve what I didn't like about my physical appearance through fashion and cosmetics, then what an easy fix compared to having to work on my inside, my character.

Amy Roloff

Beauty does come from the inside. Fashion and cosmetics just enhance what we already have. It's like a present: sometimes we look at the pretty, shiny wrapping paper and the big, fancy bow instead of being excited about what is inside the package. The ultimate gift could be wrapped in plain paper, but we're more likely to choose the gift wrapped in pretty paper. In the end, though, the character of a person will shine brighter and longer, no matter the fashion or makeup she is wearing. I worked on my character because that was what I could do instead of trying to be or look like someone else through fashion and makeup. This little achondroplastic-dwarf body is what it is, but I would make it the best I could physically. I don't wear kids' sizes, and rarely petite; I wear what I'm comfortable in and what looks good on me. Shoes are a whole different story. Anyone for flip-flops?

None of us want to start something already thinking we're going to have an uphill battle each and every time we try. Not that I expected success to be easy, but I didn't think it would always be this hard either. I felt as if no matter what I did or how hard I tried to put myself in the game with others, I would never quite be an equal to them. I was different, and it's how the world saw me—different, not equal.

The older I got, the more I realized it's not how others saw me that mattered but how I saw myself. And what I thought about myself was a roller-coaster ride. I was good enough and confident one moment, and not good enough and lacked self-confidence the next. Having an illness for a number of years didn't help either. To the world, beauty verifies our worth, but my worth was already there—I just needed to see and believe it. I didn't have celebrity posters hung up on my walls. I couldn't be like those people, so why have something that reminded me of how different I was and that I couldn't meet some perceived standard? I didn't want the reminder. No matter what, I'll always be Amy, a dwarf girl just trying to be herself.

I realized I was no exception from other young girls and women. What we looked like mattered. In the end, what finally mattered to me the most was what I thought about myself and how God saw me. Ultimately, that is what counts. My beauty needs to come from my heart, not from my outside appearance.

I wanted to blend in with others, and I tried hard to do just that so I wouldn't always be noticed as being different. Instead of finding the group of friends and community that I wanted to be a part of, I was always trying to be part of a group I thought I needed to be a part of to feel accepted. God already accepted me, and I don't know why I strayed from that.

At a young age, I came down with an unexpected illness. I was sick with this illness for about six years at a pivotal time in my growing-up years. At around nine years of age and in fourth grade, I began to lose my appetite and not be able to hold down food very well. I kept getting sick and often had diarrhea. Worrying more and more about locating a bathroom everywhere I went and making sure I could get there in time took some of my focus off what I was wearing and how makeup might have made me prettier. Being sick all the time scared me. I didn't know what foods affected me. It was a big worry and source of stress for me.

I didn't know what was happening to my body or why I kept getting sick, yet I felt that I needed to figure it out on my own; I could take care of it by myself and be the one to make it all go away. So for a long time I didn't tell my parents what was going on. It was just another thing that was wrong with me, and no one would be able to fix it, but maybe I could. If I watched what I ate and tried to understand what foods affected me, maybe it would just go away.

My illness started to affect my schoolwork, but I couldn't tell my teachers why I had to leave the classroom so often to go to the restroom. I hoped they would simply understand and let me go. What reason could I give them? "Oh sorry, I'm sick and have to leave class to use the bathroom a lot." I just said I really had to go.

After months of trying to deal with it on my own, I finally had to tell my parents. I was getting sicker and had started to bleed, and it scared me.

They were extremely worried, sad, and upset that I hadn't told them much sooner. For the first time, I saw tears well up in my mom and dad's eyes. I knew I should have let them know long before; they deserved to know because I was their daughter and they would've done anything they could to help me.

I was glad I finally told them, because this burden I had been carrying around for so long was now off my shoulders. What a tremendous relief! It was foolish for me to think I could handle this on my own. They asked me many questions: When did it start? How did I feel? Did I hurt anywhere? Did I get sick, or was I just having diarrhea? What did I eat? How often did I have to use the bathroom? Did my teacher or any friends know? They asked me to keep a journal of what I ate, how often I used the bathroom, my weight, and how I felt each day. Whew! We were on a mission to figure out how to get me better.

Now that my parents knew, I didn't have to go through this alone anymore. My dad and mom would take care of me, and everything was going to be okay. After I told them about having to leave the classroom, I got a note from my parents, and later one from my doctor, giving me permission to leave class to use the restroom anytime I needed to. This was a huge relief. I settled into a routine, and the teachers learned not to question me if I asked to leave class to use the bathroom. I couldn't wait a minute longer after I asked; I had to leave the classroom right away.

Even though having the note eased my anxiety tremendously, I missed a lot of what was talked about in class and usually ended up having more homework than the other kids. Over time, school became tougher for me academically because I missed so much class time. I worried all the time. It didn't matter where I was. Whether I was on the playground, in the classroom, walking home from school, with my family, or out and about with my friends, I was always worried about where the bathroom was. Would there be one when I really needed one? Did I hide what was wrong with me well enough so no one would ask questions? I felt bad that my parents had to worry about me all the time.

I loved playing tetherball with friends on the school playground. Surprisingly enough, I was good at it. It wasn't until some of the kids figured out to hit the ball over my head so that I couldn't reach it to hit it back that I realized I wasn't so good at it anymore. Though I didn't win as often, I still loved playing the game. It was about having fun and being with friends.

When my illness started to get worse, I often had to stop in the middle of a game or talking with friends at recess and ask the playground attendant if I could go to the bathroom. I became hesitant to get involved in things. My friends just thought I was a little weird because I seemed to always have to leave in the middle of stuff. They saw me leave the classroom and come back frequently. They saw me stop in the middle of games on the playground to leave and then come back. I would sometimes arrive late to class or come back to the playground and then recess would be over.

My illness began to affect everything I did and everywhere I went. It was frustrating, embarrassing, and I felt more isolated. Then it became my new norm, something I had to adapt to, until we knew what was going on and how to get me well.

After months of being sick, I wasn't getting better. I had to go to the bathroom so often during the day that it wore me out. I wasn't getting enough sleep because I kept waking up in the middle of the night. I began to avoid interacting with my friends at school, and I became quieter and more subdued. My parents noticed that I wasn't as happy as I used to be or as interested in doing things with my friends. They asked often if there was anything else wrong or if they could help me in any other way. How was school going? Anything going on with my friends? Was I feeling okay? I used to say things were fine, but not anymore. Something was wrong and I wanted to get better. I was sad.

After trying to figure out what was causing my illness on our own without success, my parents took me to a doctor because I was getting worse. At our first appointment, they weren't sure what was wrong either, but asked my parents and me to monitor my symptoms and document as much as I could each day. Two weeks later, we went back and I gave them the information from my journal. The doctors wanted to perform a number of tests to see what was going on in my "insides." The worst part was having to drink some awful stuff before having a colonoscopy done. As a young girl, this was miserable and scary.

A Little Me

After getting the test results back, I was diagnosed with ulcerative colitis. I would be on this roller coaster of a ride with medications and doctor appointments for quite a while before getting better. They wanted to see if they could manage the illness through medication before trying more drastic options. We thought I was too young to have this, but this illness doesn't only affect older people. We know now that many young people get this illness.

Then the roller-coaster ride began—the ups and downs of trying to see what medications worked or didn't, doctor appointments, hospital visits, tests, x-rays, and more doctor appointments to get second opinions. I was tired of having to tell the story of what was going on with me to so many different doctors when no real answers were given as to why this was happening.

One specific medication, prednisone, made me bloated and caused me to gain weight very easily. As my illness worsened, my dosage increased. Though my body seemed to respond well to the higher dosage, when I was on the full dose I put on a lot of weight and became bloated from retaining too much water. Then the doctors slowly decreased the dose to see how little could prevent another flare up of diarrhea, passing blood, dehydration, and excessive weight loss.

When I was able to get by on a lower dosage for a while, I was excited and so hopeful that I was starting to get better. But this was only temporary and didn't last long. I went from gaining ten to fifteen pounds and being puffy to losing twenty pounds and becoming very thin. I felt as if I were in a world all by myself, and I was scared. Even with my family all around me I felt alone.

The illness wreaked havoc on my body for about six years. Needless to say, the years I was ill immensely worsened my already-poor self-image, low confidence, and how "unpretty" I felt about myself. I knew my body was wearing out and wouldn't be able to handle this illness much longer.

A year after I was diagnosed with ulcerative colitis, my family had the opportunity to go on a Memorial Day family reunion vacation. It was a chance to see family we hadn't seen in quite some time. But my parents weren't sure whether to go or not since I was so sick and weak after going through another up-and-down episode with my medications. I felt so bad because it was my fault that my family might not go. In the end, they decided to go, but I would stay at my grandma's house. This was hard because I really wanted to be with my family. I missed my mom and dad, and ended up getting worse at my grandma's house. I became weak and couldn't eat, drink, or do very much. It was the last time I stayed at my grandma's; taking care of me was just too much for her.

Every youth church event, overnight sleepover, day at school, shopping excursion, bike ride, and family vacation—or just plain playing in the neighborhood—was affected by my illness. My "normal" had always been being a little person in an average-size world, but now I had a new normal: living with an illness. I adjusted to both pretty well, but my illness was sometimes harder to handle. I thought this would surely be healed, but after years of having this illness I wasn't so sure. How long was this going to go on?

The high dosage of medication I had to be on for so long eventually became a big concern. Each time my doctors tried to gradually decrease my dosage, I ended up needing more. The dosage was becoming way too high for someone my age, and the possible damage it was having on my body after all these years was a serious issue. The doctor I had been seeing for quite some time finally recommended surgery because it seemed to be the best and only other option to cure me of this disease.

My parents weren't prepared for this possibility. They were crushed that I was still sick and had had to live with this illness for the last six years. In the months and years that had gone by, my parents tried several options that had the potential of helping me to get better without surgery. They didn't rule out surgery, but wanted to do their due diligence for their baby girl before putting me through this. After going to more doctors and getting second opinions, the final recommendation was to have surgery

I had hoped to get better without surgery, but my hope began to fade as I got closer to high school age. It had already been five years of visiting doctors, hospitals, and taking medications. I needed to accept that my body was changing because of the medicine I was taking and there was nothing I could do.

Having this illness, I felt more compelled to find ways to stop comparing myself to others as well as to acknowledge my own reality. *I'm a little person with an illness that may change the rest of my life.* Wow! At fourteen, this reality was hard to take in. What exactly would change in my life after surgery? My health? I was so thankful to be as healthy and physically able as I was for a little person, but this illness—ulcerative colitis—seemed to change everything. It was tough going through my junior high years and entering high school with it. I was good at hiding my feelings and being the ever so happy-go-lucky girl. I was consistently voted the kindest and nicest person in school. I thought these were good qualities, certainly better than other things I could have been voted.

I was very good at holding on to the doctor's note that said I could leave the classroom anytime I needed to use the restroom. So if PE class became overwhelming, I'd take a break and leave class just because. If I suddenly panicked thinking I had to go right then or I'd have an accident in the classroom, I'd simply get up and go, taking a moment just to breathe and escape the difficulty. I didn't want to embarrass myself, so that note was my safety net. I didn't want my friends to find out; I didn't want them to think I was even more weird and different.

Throughout my illness, my mom took me to most of my appointments even though she was a full-time working mom. This time was special to me because my many doctor appointments gave me lots of one-on-one moments with my mom, which were like golden sunshine during this whole ordeal, brightening and softening what I was going through. I cherished these mother-daughter moments, especially shopping and going out to eat with her after my appointments. Such simple things as getting ice cream, going grocery shopping, or taking a walk in the park by the hospital were my extra-special times with my mom. Out of love for me, she was good at making our time together be about more than just my illness—that's what moms do. Whatever it took. Whatever negative thoughts I had or how unbeautiful I thought I was, my mom and dad always knew how to make me feel better. They knew I was the most beautiful when I was just being myself and not trying to be like someone else.

Those were tough years for me, but I held on to the hope that everything was going to be okay one day. And that someday finally came—but not exactly as I thought it would. My life did become much better after surgery, but remained very different than what I had expected for the rest of my life.

Eventually, after six years of seeing doctors, lots and lots of tests, being on medication that either made me bloated like a fish or turned me into a skinny girl who looked even sicker, and all the while my parents making sure I wasn't used as a guinea pig for unnecessary tests or medications, we said enough of this roller-coaster ride. My body wouldn't be able to withstand much more of the medication I was on at such a high dosage. Finally my parents agreed with the doctors: I would need to have surgery.

So in ninth grade I had surgery on Valentine's Day, an appropriate day because, as I look back now, I know my parents had a tough time making this decision but did so out of love for their daughter—me. They showed me such strong faith and the power of prayer in how they constantly prayed for strength to overcome such a trying time and for guidance in making a tough decision.

I knew God never left me, though I know I left him many, many times. His love never wavered when my faith did. I just kept thinking, *Why me? Why me?* I remember crying often at night hoping this would just go away and I would get better and back to normal. But my faith seemed to be the only thing I could hang on to, and it's what has kept me strong to this day.

The surgery changed my physical body for the rest of my life, leaving a big scar and making it necessary to wear a device. It took a few years to get used to it, but once I did my life had a new norm. I was healthy and went back to doing all the normal things I did before my illness. I was in my high school's marching band; I can enjoy swimming, cooking, riding bikes, driving, and hanging out with friends. I've been able to live a full and active life ever since, despite years of being sick. My parents remained strong during this trying time, and being able to lean on them was wonderful. Their love was tremendous.

Encouragement from Amy:

~Life isn't easy or fair all the time, but it's also not always as hard as we make it out to be. We can't expect life to always be full of joy, but we can always be happy and joyful in our hearts. Life doesn't just happen; we need to make an effort, be intentional, and keep working at it. Besides, we already have some of the tools to make life happen—desire, discipline, passion, and devotion. Don't be afraid to use them.

CHAPTER 6

Be Yourself

A Little Me

I wish I knew back then what I know today. If that were the case, of course my life would have changed and I would not be doing what I'm doing now. I was married, and now I am divorced, with four kids, an empty-nester, a grandma, still doing our reality TV show, speaking all over the country, traveling, writing, starting a blog, and have a new online business—Amy Roloff's Little Kitchen. But most importantly, my experiences and challenges, the friends I have and the many people I've met along the way have helped shaped me into who I am today, right now.

I'm sure more adventures and challenges, more life, will continue to shape me. In the end, it's up to me to make the choice to see myself as someone who matters, has value and a purpose, and is beautiful too. I don't need to let others do that for me. I will strive to keep improving and bring the best of me to all I do.

I spent many days and nights in my younger years not exactly wishing for a different life, but wishing my life were easier and more like what I saw in others' lives. As I reflect back on how I felt and how I saw myself, it was different than how I perceived others thought of me. I know, it probably doesn't make sense, but the more I converse with other women—at women's conferences, organizations, colleges, and so forth—the more I realize we often play this mind game within ourselves. What is our image, and what should our image be? How do others see us? What changes do I need to make to fit in or try to look like others? We think more about how others see us and what others think of us than of what we think about ourselves. Truly, how we perceive ourselves is often different than how people really see us.

I still sometimes struggle with body image, especially as I get older. However, I am so much more appreciative and thankful, less critical and more understanding of myself. You've got to love the wisdom and grace that come with age. When my body started to go south, I'll admit, I thought about getting some sort of plastic surgery to give the old body a little lift. After doing reality television for fifteen years and seeing so many women having it done, I guess it's no surprise that it crept into my mind. But if I change one thing, I'll probably want to change something else and then something else after that.

We are inundated with countless images suggesting that we need to change this or that to look better, more beautiful, and to get more out of life. I'm defying those odds because I believe I already have all that without changing my body. If I go there again, feeling the need to hold on to an image that pleases others, I know I'll end up on another roller-coaster ride of thinking I'm not pretty enough, worthy enough, or good enough unless I change my looks. When that happens I need to get those thoughts out of my mind as quickly as I can.

Do I really want to spend my time and financial resources changing myself because of the pressure out there to look years younger than the age I am? Nah, I want to be empowered of my own accord, instead of looking to others for empowerment or changing my looks because of societal pressure.

How about changing course from thinking we need to look as if we never age? Maybe instead be a part of the group of women for whom growing old gracefully and naturally is beautiful and acceptable. There isn't anything I can change about being a little person, but there is a whole lot I can do to keep a strong and better attitude of who I am, my worth, and the possibilities that still lie ahead. There is a certain beauty at any age, even in growing old gracefully and knowing your own worth. Just be you.

A Little Me

Like many women, I try to look and feel my best, but getting older changes everything. It's a lot of work to try to look younger than you actually are. Why do we keep looking back, thinking we lost something? Aren't we supposed to get wiser the older we get, and maybe more appreciative and thankful because we know what it took to get here? Men don't seem to have to work at it as hard or think about their appearance as much as we do.

Growing up I felt the need to try to look like other girls. The older I get, seeing my body shift and seeing what other older women feel the need to do to look years younger, the more I think this will never end. I'll fall again into the trap of feeling as though I'm playing catch-up and never quite making it. Then I try not to focus so much on what I look like or compare myself to others. Instead, again I muster up a positive attitude and affirmations to reassure myself that I'm fine just the way I am, the way I'm supposed to look. I do a lot of good, and my heart means well, but what I look like continues to matter to me because it impacts so many aspects of my life—socially and professionally. I just want to run from it sometimes.

Don't get me wrong, I like to feel beautiful and try to look beautiful, but most of all I try to be beautiful *inside* and out. Beauty changes, and being beautiful on the inside isn't dependent on the outside. I like the saying that beauty is in the eye of the beholder. Beauty and body image should not rest with someone else's perception but in how we perceive ourselves. Just because someone doesn't like the "art" doesn't mean the art isn't of value or doesn't have beauty.

The older I get the wiser I'm becoming because I'm liking myself more rather than having what others think matter more. I won't ever be able to please everyone, and not everyone is going to think I'm beautiful either. Besides, I'd rather have my heart and my character speak louder about who I am and my beauty than my outward appearance. Isn't that the essence of someone's true beauty?

Yep, I struggled with body image for a long time, and still do but to a lesser degree. I didn't have a very good perception of myself as a person, let alone as a little person. I was different, and being the only one different in my family, among my friends, and pretty much anywhere I went in life made me feel out of place. I never quite seemed to feel a part of anything. Even though I tried so hard to be liked by everyone and to like everyone in return, it wouldn't have mattered anyway if others thought I was wonderful, because I didn't feel it within myself. How I saw and felt about myself did matter to me, but I didn't realize how much it mattered at the time in order to stop that kind of thinking.

The negative image I already had got magnified during the six years of my illness, continuing after surgery. My body image changed even more as a result, and now I really had something to serve as a constant reminder that my body was a little more unbeautiful—a big, long scar. Looking back at pictures taken during my illness, I sometimes see sadness in my eyes, even though I was smiling. I remember trying to hide so many of my feelings and emotions, to come across as strong and confident, but inside I didn't feel that way, and I don't think I did as great a job of hiding my feelings as I thought I did.

I slowly built up a wall around myself that became like a fortress for hiding my feelings, thoughts, and emotions from my family and friends. I didn't let anyone in. I didn't let anyone get to know Amy. I wanted them to see the image I thought they wanted to see of me on the outside, not get to know the real me inside, from my heart. Wouldn't trying to be the best on the outside be good enough? If they liked me on the outside, maybe I could slowly let them get to know me on the inside. I hoped that everyone would simply see me as this fun-loving, adventurous, strong, confident, happy-go-lucky girl and it wouldn't matter anymore how different I looked.

I was only fooling myself. I've come to realize that when I hide myself from others and think they are seeing what I want them to see, I'm the one who has a different perspective. I wasn't the open, expressive, confident, strong girl I thought they were seeing. I was standoffish, a little cold, quiet, and too serious, and ended up isolating myself from others. Yes, I was involved in many activities with friends and at school, but sometimes we can be in the same place as others and yet keep ourselves from being a part of it as well. The real me got a little lost, and I didn't know exactly who I really was or who I wanted to be anymore, nor did a lot of my friends.

I would often wait for friends to call and ask me to hang out or go do something. I wasn't usually the one to initiate or plan an activity with other people. Instead, I would sit at home alone and wonder why no one called. In high school I would go to school on Mondays and hear my friends' fun stories of bike rides, mall shopping, movies, or ball games followed by ice cream. I felt left out because I let fear hold me back, fear of rejection and of hearing "no." I made it a lot more about the *no*, feeling as if others were making up excuses for why I wasn't invited, because I was different. I made it about me instead of about friendship.

Looking back, I'm not sure I would have hung out with me. I probably wasn't that much fun a lot of the time. No way could it have been that they just didn't want to; it had to be because I was different, a little person, something I couldn't change. I didn't give them a chance to ask or a reason to include me in the conversation, because I had already made up my mind and written myself off before they could possibly say anything else. I didn't just think about the what-ifs, I made the what-ifs a reality.

Yeah, the perception we have of ourselves can get us all twisted up. My faith kept me on my feet, though, and gave me the strength to remind myself that I was worthy. I'm beautifully and wonderfully made; we all are. God gave us his greatest gift—love and life with him.

I would often say to myself when I was younger, *Why me? Why is this happening to me? Why am I a little person? Why does life seem hard and challenging all the time? Why am I sick? Why doesn't anyone like me?*

Then God would give me another day to get a grip on myself and say, *Enough of this kind of talk.* I have an opportunity to realize it's not about my being a little person, it's about trusting him in the life he has given me. It's about being kind to myself so I can be kind to others. It's about my attitude. It's about being grateful, appreciative, and thankful in any situation I'm in and for what I do have, what I can do, and getting outside of myself instead of focusing on me and what I think isn't going right. I needed to realize how and what I think about myself does matter but thinking about others matters too, sometimes even more. I know I've often made things more complicated and challenging than they actually were.

So what that I don't look like a certain celebrity, or like my friends, or that I can't wear a certain style of fashion? *So what* that the cosmetics I wear don't put me in the top-ten-most-fabulous-looking-women list? *So what* that I'm different? We're all different, and deep down I didn't want everyone to look like me and I really didn't want to look like anyone else. I was struggling with me and knew I needed to work on my beauty from the inside out, not the outside in.

A Little Me

Many people try so hard to be different, to stand out and be noticed, and what did I do? I tried to blend in and be like everyone else instead of appreciating my difference and taking advantage of it. All because my self-image and the lopsided messaging I fed myself were not affirming. Why did I spend so much time waiting for other people's approval when I couldn't even give it to myself? I had blinders on. The many people to meet, the friends I had, and the life that was out there, waiting—I didn't see it the way I should have. I was too worried about what I saw in the mirror. On one hand, I really did like what I saw, but on the other, my focus changed when I walked out the front door. I allowed fear and negative thoughts about myself to cause havoc in my mind.

I'm good enough, but then I'm not. I can do this, but I can't. I'm beautiful, but not like the other girls. What happens if I fail?

Okay, okay, enough of that self-doubt talk. My mind-set wasn't strong enough to turn it off or turn it around to ask, *What if I succeed? What if I'm really good at it? Why not give it a try? What if I fail but pick myself up and try again and make it? I am beautiful.*

Now that I'm older and have lived life a little, I'm amazed that some of these feelings I had as a young girl still come filtering back into my mind. *Can I really do this?* Yep, my self-image and how I saw myself compared to what I saw all around me affected how I perceived my self-worth, and my self-confidence.

I remember getting ready for school one day when I was in fourth grade. I really wanted to wear this one outfit, a blue jumper with red hearts all over it, because I loved it, I thought I looked great in it, and it was a cool outfit. I wore a red long-sleeved shirt underneath and little black shoes. It was a cool, rainy spring day with big, billowing clouds that allowed the sun to peak through and shine every once in a while.

Well, my mom told me I had to wear my rain boots to school. For some crazy reason, I did not want to wear those rain boots. My friends wouldn't be wearing rain boots, and I wanted to be like everyone else. Why did I have to wear rain boots? They weren't as cool back then as they seem to be now—colorful, with polka dots and all kinds of fun designs and styles.

Since my elementary school wasn't far from my house, I walked to school. My mom was usually late leaving for work, and so I waited and waited in my room for her to leave, pretending to be getting ready for school. Finally, she left for work. I quickly took off my boots, put my shoes on, and ran out the front door so I wouldn't be late for school. I stuffed my boots in the bush by the front porch. When I came home from school I had to make it look as though I had worn my boots to school, and I was afraid my mom would come home early or our housekeeper would tell my mom if she found out what I had done, so I hid my boots in the bush.

I felt so proud of myself because I was going to look like everyone else. No boots. I was a happy-go-lucky kid that day. The thing was, there were a lot more kids wearing rain boots that day than not. Maybe their moms had told them they had to as well. I still felt more like one of the cool kids, instead of always being the different kid. I splashed through puddles and my tights got wet, but I didn't care. It was fun. I had worn my favorite outfit and my favorite shoes. I felt more like a part of my group of friends, and I hadn't been jokingly laughed at because my mom made me wear uncool rain boots to school.

A Little Me

Such a simple moment about something so small made me feel good about myself. Why? Maybe because it was daring to disobey my mom, though she was right. Maybe it was a chance to get outside my box a little and not restrict what I could or couldn't do. I'm not sure, but this little moment was one of many seemingly small moments that contributed to the formation of my self-image and feelings of belonging during my growing-up years and into my young-adult life.

This was just about the time I began to get sick. Of course it was an illness I wanted to hide from everyone I knew. However, the medication I was on didn't always allow me to do that. I had a hard time explaining to the other kids and my friends what was going on when my physical appearance changed. I wanted to try to hide it because it was yet another thing I felt was wrong with me, that made me different. But I had to say something, so I blamed how I looked on the medication, which caused me to be so thin at one point and bloated another. If fashion and cosmetics weren't going to help me have a better image of myself, it was easier to blame it on the medication.

I wasted a lot of time placing the source of my self-confidence in other people's opinions. One little comment, gesture, or whisper, or body language that may have been innocent enough, and I blew it out of proportion in all sorts of directions. Life truly happens when I can get outside of the box I'm stuck in.

A friend recently showed me a meme that spoke volumes to me.

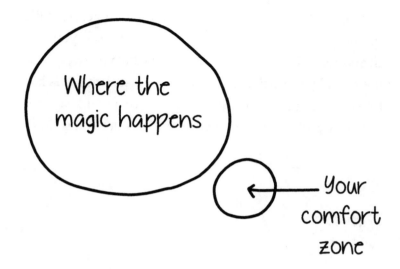

From the time I was school aged to college and young-adult life, I got stuck on comparing myself to others around me. I listened to others who told me, "This is what beauty looks like." That faulty belief limited my mobility in regards to what I thought I could do more than any difference or physical limitation may have. When I allowed my mind and thoughts to believe in something that wasn't real, I couldn't see the beauty I had inside, which in turn would have helped me see how truly capable and beautiful I was. When our minds and hearts are honest and true to ourselves, we can make magic happen. If we believe what others think and the negative stuff out there, we stay in our comfort zones and don't venture out into the possibilities.

Encouragement from Amy:

~ Attitude is everything. A bad attitude changes your life in one direction, and a positive attitude changes your life in another direction. You can choose what you want your life to be by the attitude you hold. Repeat: attitude is key to everything in your life. A negative one will keep you down. A positive one has the potential to let you soar.

CHAPTER 7

Beauty and
Relationships

A Little Me

After all these years, I'm still amazed at how I perceived myself in my younger years, but I'm even more amazed at how I failed to see the real me. The image I had of myself was not always a good one and played havoc on my self-confidence and feelings of worth and purpose. I put a lot of internal pressure on myself when it came to beauty and my outside package.

Instead of seeing Amy, what I often saw was how much I did not look like anyone else. So up went the hand telling me I had to stop here because, no matter what I did to beautify myself, this was the best I could do. No matter what I did, or how badly I wanted to, I would never look like "that."

When it came to my appearance, the images I saw in magazines and how my friends as well as others looked were my barometer, but I never seemed to measure up to what I strived for. I was always trying to keep up with everyone else, and that was a daunting task, which took up way too much of my valuable time and thinking. That's why I know my faith will forever be my saving grace. I could have given up long ago, but I didn't. My faith kept me going from day to day even though I felt like I didn't measure up and would never be good enough.

So *what* if I didn't think I was beautiful or look like I thought I should or wanted to? I placed unrealistic standards on myself, which I allowed to come from magazines, media, television, and society as a whole instead of from what my faith told me. God had already told me I was worthy and beautiful. We are all uniquely, beautifully, and wonderfully made, one of a kind. I don't have the right to give up, and I don't have the right to say to God that what he created isn't good enough. Yes, my faith was and is my saving grace. So when I placed more importance on other people's opinions and the messages of unattainable beauty I was absorbing, I did a disservice to myself. I didn't give myself due credit, and it hampered me from giving and doing my best.

I'm in what I call my second act of life right now. My life has changed so much more than I ever expected. I've faced challenges from my own doing as well as from living life as a little person.

In my second act I have faced two big challenges so far: divorce and being an empty-nester. The thought of ever being in another relationship fell flat on the floor; it was never going to happen, because feelings I had growing up about beauty and worth came rushing back to the forefront of my mind. *I'm not going to date again. No one is going to find me attractive enough to date.* But I was reminded that the outside package isn't the only thing people look at. A person's character, personality, and heart can overshadow the outside package.

The question I find myself still asking, even at this age, is, *Is being different, and how it affects my beauty, going to be a big factor again in my life?* I hope that, being this age, in my fifties, it won't play such a big part in my life as it did in my early years. We shall see.

My second act has shown me it's still a wonderful life, even with challenges. Surrounding myself with a good community of people who like me and help me see the real, wonderful me and help me work through some of my challenges, there hasn't been a dull moment.

It does matter how and what we think about ourselves, because when we truly like ourselves we can see how amazingly our beauty shines outward. Be kind to yourself and acknowledge your inner beauty, and then use the freedom from that to give kindness to others and see all the beauty around you.

A Little Me

***

In high school I began to have crushes on boys and stress over who liked me and who might not. Who did I dare like? What others saw when they looked at me was a dwarf, a little person, who was short in stature with short legs and arms. I couldn't possibly like someone and they me in that kind of way. I allowed people to stop there, on the outside, instead of getting to know me as the person I was on the inside; I was too scared to let people see that part of me.

I was happy and fun-loving, but following my surgery, I was still self-conscious and still compared myself to others. I hoped no one would notice how my body had changed from surgery, not just my scar but a body that, although certainly better internally, was a little more different on the outside. I just tried to do my best to appear as beautiful as I could on the outside, but I didn't let anyone get to know the real me. Opening up that part of me on the inside and letting people in was just too vulnerable.

My thoughts, ideas, dreams, hopes, and fears . . . you know, the important stuff about someone—these are the things that really connect people to each other. They form a big part of how strong friendships and relationships begin. You can't have good, meaningful friendships if only one person is taking the risks to open up and be vulnerable. Frankly, I was too focused on myself and didn't take into consideration that it's hard for others to open up and be vulnerable as well.

The only people who knew about my surgery and how I felt about it were my family and a few close friends—that's it. I kept my community of people small, though I wanted people to like me and I hoped for a personal relationship one day. But how could that happen if I didn't let others get to know me? I kept myself too guarded for any of that to happen easily.

I thought having a personal relationship was never going to be a part of my life. My insecurities didn't keep me from having boy crushes in high school, but I did think *why*? I didn't want to get hurt, but no one does when they open themselves up to another. I didn't want to see the look of surprise, the look of "I didn't know that about you," before they walked away. So my expectations of certain things, like marriage and having a family of my own, became distant thoughts.

And yet the glimmer of hope of *maybe one day* never completely left my mind. That's the thing about hope and dreaming the seemingly impossible: there is always a possibility of our dreams coming true. I couldn't give up hope on anything. We just need a little confidence and to believe with some determination to make it happen.

When girls get together, what do they talk about? Boys. When my girlfriends and I got together, I'd hear their stories of liking this boy or that one, going to dances, and of boys asking if they could walk them to class or go out after school and so on. There were no cell phones, social media, or anything like that back then, so interacting with others face-to-face was the good, old-fashioned way we interacted.

Girlfriends would ask me to pass messages to boys for them, hoping to get a message back in return. I was the go-between, like playing the game Telephone. I was the messenger but not the one receiving a message from a boy who liked me.

I didn't have anything to contribute to the conversation when we talked about boys, and I was too scared to admit that I liked a boy.

But I liked listening to their stories and laughing and being silly with them because it made me a part of something. I didn't talk to my friends about liking a boy because I didn't want to risk being laughed at or for the boy to say, "No way." I didn't want to face that kind of rejection and look like a fool in front of my girlfriends. It was too scary and embarrassing to me. I was too worried about what others thought of me instead of thinking about what I wanted.

The perception I had of my appearance and how it affected having relationships seemed to follow me everywhere I went. I couldn't shake it off. It was like an irritating fly I kept swatting at but could never seem to squash. Sometimes I saw the fly and sometimes I just heard it, but either way, it was always there.

I didn't date in high school or college. I saw dating as a bridge to be crossed to officially make it into the "you are somebody" group. I may have gone to a dance or two, but I wouldn't call it *dating*. There was a dance in junior high, and I thought no way was anyone going to ask me to it. *That doesn't happen to me.* Although I didn't talk to a lot of boys, it wasn't because I didn't want to; I was way too shy and uncomfortable to do so. Sure, I would talk to boys if they were in my class, in a group setting, or somewhere it was safe or necessary, but I didn't just go up to boys and start talking with them "just because" or if I liked them. That would have been too scary.

A few days before the actual dance, as I listened to my friends talk about getting their dresses, the boys who had asked them, and all of that other girl talk, I sat quietly and just listened. What could I possibly contribute to this conversation? Nothing. I wasn't going. I dreamt about being asked and what I would wear. What would the boy look like? I was still sick in junior high school, so I would blame not getting asked to school dances or boys not liking me on my illness. I loved hearing all the fun stories about the dances from my friends the next day.

But magic happens when we allow ourselves to believe and step outside of our comfort zone, and to my surprise, magic happened this time. I got asked to go to the dance by a boy. I had talked to him often enough before and thought he was pretty cute and nice, and he was tall. Then again, everyone is tall to me, but he truly was tall. My immediate thoughts of course were, *Why? Why are you asking me to go?* Oh, who cares why? I was excited! My mom took me shopping for a new dress. It was light blue and flowy, and I loved it because I could twirl in it. To this day, I still love a dress I can twirl in. I spent the next several days altering and hemming my dress so I could wear it to the dance.

My date and I met at school, where the dance was being held. When he walked up to me he gave me a wrist corsage, my first corsage, and it was beautiful. I thanked him, and we engaged in a little small talk. The funny thing was, we were both shy, so we ended up not talking or dancing much at all. We were simply there together. I didn't know how to dance with someone that much taller than me, and he didn't know what to do either. I'm sure we looked a little awkward together. I knew I needed to get over that if I hoped someone else would. Most of the time we just stood around listening to the music and talking to our friends. I danced with him for a dance or two, and then it was over. The night went by so quickly that it didn't feel real to me. I had let my romantic imagination run away from me, imagining what the experience would feel and look like.

Thinking of how this boy had the guts to ask me to the dance, I laugh at it now and still get a smile on my face. I'm not sure I would have asked me considering how shy I was. It was the beginning of lifting the veil for me, realizing someone could see something more in me than I saw in myself. It was a small step, but that's all it takes: a small step that leads to something else and to better things.

I was thrilled that everything went great that night and my illness hadn't gotten in the way; it made me feel a little happier about myself. I had experienced a real-life, fun, teenage-girl moment without everyday life or my illness getting in the way. I felt like a princess, and then it was gone: a moment I still remember with fondness. A boy had asked me to go to a dance. I would not be asked to another dance again all through high school, including my high school prom, and college. I went to many dances, but I didn't get asked.

Dating is such a touchstone in high school life; it impacts, positively or negatively, how we see and feel about ourselves. It did for me anyway. Since I didn't really date, how I viewed my appearance was reinforced. I felt as if I didn't have beauty.

When I get together with girlfriends now, we reminisce and say, "I remember when . . ." Just the other day I was with some girlfriends and the conversation reminded us of our high school dating days. We ended up telling stories about those days, I listened, and eventually they ended up talking about the second marriages they're now in, the years they have been together, how they met, and about relationships in general. It was fascinating to me because I'm now dating for the very first time in my life. I was reliving a little of my high school days, hearing their stories, and from a perspective I had never experienced. Wow! It was wonderful to laugh with them and not worry about having a story to share.

I sometimes regret hanging on way too long to the need to be liked by everyone, to be that perfect friend, and wanting to be a girlfriend, so that I ended up missing out on a lot of coming-of-age teen-age experiences I could have looked back on and laughed about now; experiences from which I could have learned a lot more about others and about myself. I'm not saying you have to date in high school in order to have wonderful experiences and a positive perception of yourself. For me, dating was yet one more thing I didn't get to experience like everyone else did. I put myself on the sidelines of life a lot instead of living it, something that had a lasting impact.

Another dance back in high school was the Sadie Hawkins dance, and this time the girls were supposed to ask the boys to go. *Should I dare ask someone?* I knew how I felt when a boy had asked me: excited, happy, and thrilled he took a chance on asking someone who was different without worrying how his friends would react. I always felt like the forever-friend, not the girl a boy wants as his girlfriend. So I dared myself and found enough courage and confidence to push away any self-doubts I had and asked a boy to this dance. I was so nervous. I can remember my heart pounding and how I wanted to run away. I just wanted to stay inside my comfort zone, but instead I took this moment to jump outside of my comfort zone and mustered up enough courage to take the risk and ask a boy to the dance.

I was between classes and thought this would be a good time to do it. There was enough time to talk if we wanted to, but not so much time to make it awkward if there were a lot of his friends around, in case he said no. How embarrassing that would be. I wanted an escape route in case I suddenly wanted to crawl underneath a rock and wish this moment hadn't ever happened. Even with so many thoughts swirling around in my head, I got up enough nerve to quickly ask him. It seemed to take forever for him to respond . . . That drawn-out moment was so quiet I could hear a clock tick inside of me. I heard him say, "Thanks for asking me, but I'm already going with someone else."

What?

I hadn't thought about this possible outcome, so I just said okay and quickly walked away. Now, why hadn't this option crossed my mind instead of just two potential answers, a yes or a no? I was too late, so busy worrying about the *no* that I missed the opportunity. My heart dropped and my confidence, which I had gathered up hoping he would say yes, fell to the floor fast. It was hard to take a chance and ask, but I was so glad I did, and I thought, *Well, at least he didn't just flat-out say no. He had a reason.* So a couple of girlfriends and I went without dates and hung out with each other.

The beginning of learning how to take risks starts with courage. Courage is taking risks without knowing if you'll succeed. It may not always get easier, but gaining confidence comes with courage.

Even though I was crushed because it didn't turn out the way I had hoped, I was also proud of myself for taking the chance instead of talking myself out of it, as I had done so many times before. Success doesn't come because we think about it. Success in life comes because we have courage to take action, even if we have to do it again and again and again until we get it right. When that "right" happens it's wonderful. Life is full of ups and downs, successes and failures. Asking a boy to a dance was an emotional win because I saw that, even though I'm physically different, I am just like everyone else in so many other ways.

Summoning enough confidence and courage and then taking this simple, personal risk wasn't enough of a realization for me to throw worry, fear, and self-doubt out the window, but it was enough to prove I did have the courage to take risks again. The experience of taking some risks needs to start somewhere, and for me it began when I decided to ask a boy to a dance. Taking some risks helped me see what I could actually do. It's great when things turn out the way we thought they would, but it's also okay when they don't. Because the simple act of asking a boy to a dance was more about pushing fear away, ignoring doubt and the fear of rejection, building up my confidence, getting outside my comfort zone, and not allowing those things to continue to take over. It felt liberating when I was able to let go of all those things. I had to learn how to let go more often.

What was partly responsible for getting me through my high school years, all of that worrying, wanting to be like someone else, and lack of confidence, were music and cooking. I loved music even though I didn't think I was very good at it. I loved singing in the choir at church and playing the clarinet in the school band. Music stretched my creativity, took me into a different space than always focusing on being different, helped me to learn how to be vulnerable in a different way, and was empowering. It helped me to think a little more outside the box.

Then there was cooking. Both of my parents worked, so my family life allowed me to explore cooking. Music and cooking were about giving and sharing my passion and talent with others. Whether I was good at them or not, I didn't see either as a negative reflection on myself, perhaps because I had a genuine passion for both. I let my feelings of wanting to belong and not be so different from others take center stage in my thoughts too much, but music and cooking were like gifts I enjoyed that allowed me to focus more on giving and sharing with others. I used music and cooking to speak for me, instead of my self-doubt and fear.

A Little Me

I was fortunate that music was offered in my school, and in fifth grade I took a music class and started off by learning to play the recorder. We learned to read music, we practiced, and hopefully at the end of the class we would all be able to play the music piece together in class. I loved it. I got to take that little recorder home and practice and practice the music every day. I even came up with my own music. Let's just say I knew I probably wouldn't become a professional musician, but it was thrilling to dream about it.

I decided to continue with music and learned how to play the clarinet. I'm not really sure why I picked this instrument, since it was the longest instrument I could have chosen. How on earth was I going to learn to play an instrument that was half my size? I could have picked a more manageable instrument like the piccolo. Nope, I had made my choice and was determined to play the clarinet and play it the best I could. And that I did.

Over the next few years, I played well enough to be a part of my school concerts. Eventually, I needed to try out for band. In my junior year in high school, a good friend of mine tried out for the symphony band and made it. She wanted me to join her, but I didn't make it through the first tryouts. She begged me to give it another chance, and said that we would practice together after school so I would have a better chance of making it the next time. I was hesitant. I didn't want to fail again, and I was satisfied with staying in concert band.

I had a tendency to give up too quickly when I didn't succeed at something the first time, and it was hard to work up the confidence and courage to try again, but having my friend's support was enough encouragement for me to give it another try. We worked together almost every day after school, playing different kinds of music that were harder and more complicated than I was used to playing.

Then the day arrived, and I was so nervous. Would all the practice be enough? When it was my turn I went in, played several pieces of music that were given to me, and then left the room. It was over just like that. Now the waiting game began. After several days, I got a phone call from my band teacher letting me know I had made it into the symphony band. The results of the tryouts were listed on the band room door the next day. I wasn't at the top of the list, but I wasn't last either. There were only twelve open slots, and I had the third spot. I was so excited and happy that my friend had been so willing to help me achieve my goal. I had done it!

After having surgery in ninth grade, a few things opened up for me that I hadn't thought possible because of my illness. In my sophomore year I decided to try out for the marching band. Not realizing what it would take to be in marching band, it ended up being more of a challenge than I expected. Though my parents never discouraged me from going after things I wanted to do, they always gave me realistic input. I appreciated their being real with me. One thing I didn't consider was how I was going to keep up with the rest of the marching band. I couldn't let my little legs keep me from staying in formation. It wouldn't look good if the spectators saw this one little person out of sync with everyone else. I didn't know what I was going to do until it happened. I'd wing it.

Another challenge I encountered was the marching band uniform. It was big, heavy, and would need altering. My parents said they would talk to whomever they needed to if I were told I couldn't modify the uniform. Even if they had to buy a new uniform, they would do that for me. By telling me they would do whatever needed to be done, they showed me they were always in my corner; I wasn't alone.

A Little Me

Sometimes, if I really wanted to accomplish something important to me, I just needed to push myself to go the extra mile and make it happen. The marching band practiced all summer long to get ready for football season and a few parades during the school year. It was a lot of work on hot summer days, and a number of kids dropped out because it was hard and they were missing out on some of their summer fun. I was determined to stick it out. I did all I could to keep up and stay in formation. The band director and many of the kids were amazed at how well I did. I felt a lot of respect from everyone, and more importantly, I gained more respect for myself. Part of it was finding something I wanted to go after, which took my focus off of myself. And I was doing something fun that gave other people enjoyment too.

The trick I finally figured out was not to play when I marched. When we were standing still in formation I played the music, but when we marched I stopped playing in order to focus on keeping up. It was harder for me to march and play at the same time. Since everyone took much bigger steps than I did and the clarinet was so long and kept hitting my mouth, I decided it was more important to keep up, stay in formation, and only play the music when we stopped than to play while marching. I was thrilled to have figured out how I could march and play in my own way and be a part of something I loved along with many of my friends.

Music remained a huge part of my life—from singing in the choir in church from first grade all the way through college to listening to music, singing along with the radio in my bedroom and in the shower, and going to a lot of local concerts. I even briefly formed a neighborhood band in my younger years. We played in a friend's garage and put on concerts where we charged fifty cents. These were the moments that kept inspiring me to do much more than I thought I could.

My other main interest, cooking, which has had a big impact on my life, came about late in junior high school. One of my favorite Christmas presents I received as a young girl was a play kitchen set. I would always pretend I had guests over, with my dolls and stuffed animals serving as important guests, and had to make something very special for them to eat. I would play with that kitchen set for hours. I would go through food magazines and look at all the recipes and recreate them or change them to suit myself. I'm pretty much a self-made chef, a home chef, really.

After years of coming home from work or school activities at different times, our family didn't like eating dinner so late anymore. My dad asked us girls to help Mom out by taking turns making dinner, and my mom really appreciated the help during the week. At first my two older sisters took turns, but they really didn't like this "chore" and they were often out and about, so I soon took over making dinner. I discovered that I really liked cooking, so I began to learn what cooking really meant. Back then, packaged meals were the in thing, such as Hamburger Helper, Minute Rice, canned or frozen foods, boxed mac and cheese, and so many other quick packaged items that didn't take much prep. I started off making dinner from these, but I eventually learned how to cook real food from scratch.

I loved watching the few cooking shows that were on TV then, like Julia Child's show. I was constantly going through magazines looking for recipes to try out. I tore them out and kept them in a binder or wrote them in a recipe journal. So it's no wonder that one of my favorite classes in high school was home economics, especially the cooking unit. After a while I began coming up with my own recipes and meals, with my father and brother serving as my guinea pigs. My father would always tell me the food I cooked was good, fabulous, delicious, even if it wasn't. He said as long as it didn't move, it was good. The food I made may not have always been tasty, but he wouldn't die from it—maybe just his taste buds. If I could tell from the expression on my dad's face that he didn't like something, I would rework the recipe and have him try it again.

My friends got used to me only being able to hang out with them in the evenings or catch up on the phone instead of always right after school. As I got older, I began to have a few of my friends over for small get-togethers so I could make them dinner. They were so impressed with my cooking that others wanted to be invited to my get-togethers as well. I didn't make anything fancy; it was just good home cooking. I began to call what I love to do "gathering around the table." There is just something I really love about making a meal for others and gathering around the table to share food and conversation.

I made a very special meal after graduating from high school for three of my friends who enlisted in the military and would be leaving soon. I wanted to do this before we all went our separate ways. I felt as though I was making them their last homemade goodbye meal, because most likely we wouldn't see each other for quite some time. I can still remember what I made for them: chicken cordon bleu, wild rice, tossed salad, and homemade chocolate cake. I was excited to give and share something I could do from the heart. We laughed, shared memories of fun times, and made plans to get together again when they got out or were on leave. I think we all knew times were changing and we might not see each other again, but I took this moment to heart and never forgot about it or them. My friends left for the military the following week. That night instilled in me even more love for cooking and the importance of gathering around the table to share with those we care about and love. It is one of the simple things I loved most growing up in my family.

I loved the combination of food, people, gathering around the family dinner table, and conversation. And, boy, did my family have some doozies! We didn't always agree, and the conversations could become quite heated. That was the beautiful thing: we didn't have to agree, but we were still family that loved each other, and after we left the table everything went back to normal. We always had dinner together, though, no matter what. The meal I made for my friends before they left felt like a one-of-a-kind moment because the next time we gathered everything would be new and different, but also like coming home together. It was what I had with my family; gathering around the table was a way to catch up with everyone—even though as teenagers all we wanted to do was rush through dinner so we could go back outside as quickly as possible to hang out with our friends. The older I got, the more I wanted to hang out around the table longer with everyone.

I still look upon those times with great fondness. As much as I may not have appreciated or had as much confidence in myself when I walked outside my front door to face the world, cooking, eating, and gathering around the dinner table with my family gave me a sense of belonging and an opportunity to express myself.

I learned a lot from my dad, mom, older sisters, and younger brother at the dinner table. It was okay not to always agree on everything or not to have everyone like everything about me. That didn't mean they stopped loving me. It showed me that disagreements happen in relationships and friendships, but by talking to each other, these bonds have a chance to grow and get stronger. My brother and I often sat in awe through those conversations. It was even more fun during the holidays when we would all get together with my relatives and sit around the table for dinner and hang around afterward during dessert.

Over time I realized, and was so grateful for, how music and cooking took my focus off of being different and allowed me to think more clearly about something I did rather than what I was: a dwarf. I was learning how to become a part of things, and not for the sake of whether others liked me or not. I was doing things because I liked doing them. I was getting to know more about myself so I could be a better person, not only to myself but to everyone around me as well. Ever so slowly, I was learning that my life and who I am can't revolve so much around what others think.

I'm a person who just happens to be an achondroplastic dwarf. I wish I could have held that statement in my mind while growing up instead of always making being a dwarf a "thing." I wasted a lot of time making it an issue. Plain and simple: how I saw myself was different than how many of my friends and other people around me saw me.

My dwarfism, my self-image and how I thought about myself in comparison to how I thought others saw me, still catches up with me to this very day, and I still allow it to get in my way sometimes. Crazy, I know. It doesn't seem to matter how old I get, past experiences and thoughts seem to creep back into my mind about my value, my purpose, and whether I still matter. As others say so often, history repeats itself, just in a different way.

However, I know how to handle it better now, and those negative thoughts come and go much more quickly instead of hanging around. I'm more content with who I am and where I'm at right now. My faith strengthens my confidence, and the support, encouragement, and love I have from family and friends have helped me be a better person today than what I thought of myself back then. I made it because I had something to hang on to: my faith.

It has often comforted me to think back to when my father told me God doesn't make mistakes. Because of that, I'm here today. I'm glad to know and am forever grateful that there is someone bigger than me—God. There are things we can change, and there are things we can't, but life is always full of possibilities. I just needed to put action to those possibilities. I'm still learning how to focus not on things I can't change, like being a dwarf and what people may think about me, but on what I can change. I can only make changes within myself and do my best to manage my thoughts of inadequacy or insecurity. Regardless, not comparing myself to others continues to be hard for me, but I've gotten better at letting go and giving myself more positive affirmations.

Life does go on.

Encouragement from Amy:

~It's okay to be, and to allow yourself to be, vulnerable. It's not always easy, but in the end, it's worth it more often than not. You're not weak when you do. You have more courage when you allow yourself to open up your life and heart to more possibilities than you ever imagined.

CHAPTER 8

A First Date

I could not have imagined going through and coming out of one of the toughest personal challenges in my life—divorce—feeling happier and better about myself as a person, having grown in so many ways, and full of hope. With a few more uncertainties than I expected, my second act has definitely started off differently, yet it's also going really well. I'm no longer living the life I lived for so long. I'm no longer the active mom of young children or a wife; now I'm an empty-nester and a grandma. How did time fly by so fast and things change so much?

Looking back to my non-dating high school days, I may not have experienced the typical young girl's high school life, but I had some great friends and came through it strong enough to face the personal challenges that came my way. One of the milestones of those years was meeting other individuals with dwarfism. I did feel alone and unsure of myself sometimes when I was with other little people, because I wasn't around others like myself very often. I wanted to know what they thought, how they felt about themselves, and what they did. I wanted them to share everything with me; however, I didn't think being open and vulnerable applied to me the same way it did to them. I know it was ridiculous to think that way, but it was a fearful thing for me to do, to take that risk.

Leaving my high school years behind and entering college, I was hopeful that things would be clearer to me. My narrow mind-set on how I saw myself and how I thought others saw me began to open up a little wider, changing my perspective on life's possibilities. So what changed? I grew up. It's funny how experiences and challenges in life can help you grow up. Thank goodness!

It took quite some time to be able to believe and say to myself, *I am good, I feel stronger and better as a woman because of the per-*

sonal challenges I've faced. Those growing-up years helped me face today's challenges in a better and hopefully much healthier way. I haven't always overcome them, but I still look at many of the personal challenges I've encountered as opportunities. I've learned to take advantage of some of them, and other times they've slipped through my fingers. I'm not saying I was always perfect or I didn't kick myself and say, *Why did you do that or let that go?* However, I learned to pick myself up, start over again, and push some of those thoughts and feelings of low self-esteem aside when they start creeping in. I'm glad I woke up from the cloud I seemed to keep over me of not believing in myself enough.

So when I allowed negative thoughts, like, *I'm not good enough. You'll never do that as well as someone else will, Amy, so why try? You're wasting your time. They'll always be prettier and better than you are,* to enter my mind I would just say, *Stop it! You can't keep doing this to yourself. It's more often you saying you can't or you aren't pretty or good enough than anyone else.* I would put the brakes on and ask myself what was going on that was making me think like that again. When I'd start going down that road I'd take a step back and really take a look at what was around me, what challenge I was facing, what was hurting or making me feel less than my true self or anyone else. I'd breathe and start having more positive and realistic expectations and tell myself more positive affirmations. Maybe it was faith knocking on the door to remind me again that I was still good enough regardless of what I or anyone else thought.

The war inside my mind about my self-worth doesn't have quite as strong a hold on me as it did in my younger years, though some of the old self-doubts I had didn't completely go away and have a tendency to creep back and linger in my thoughts. If worrying about something then didn't help, why waste any more time thinking about it now? I made it over the hump. Whew! I'm tired of fear, worry, guilt, shame, comparing myself to others, and listening to social media about appearance. I didn't truly feel worthy then, but now that I'm in my fifties, it seems as though I should know by now that I am worthy. I didn't need to change then, and I'm not going to go down the road of thinking I need to change now because I'm older and my body looks different with age. It never lets up. I want to age well, and part of doing that is not thinking I need to look thirty when I'm in my fifties.

I will admit, having been filming my reality TV show and being in the media for quite some time, I've had to fight wanting to change or "fix" this or that about myself. It wears you down. Now I stop and ask, *Why are you going down that road again and doing that?* When Bruno Mars came out with his song "Just the Way You Are" I thought, *Yeah! I am amazing, and maybe one day someone else, besides me, will think I'm amazing too.* The song reminded me I need to like myself and I don't need to wait until someone else does.

Regardless of what I may be going through, I still need to find my "happy," that happy that stays with me so I don't view everything in life from a negative perspective. My happy comes from the deep-down joy I get from my faith. That kind of joy doesn't come from my thoughts and opinions or from others, but from faith because it's not based on circumstances. My faith helps me to appreciate my uniqueness and not feel so alone, scared, or inadequate. I'm beautiful and wonderfully made by the one who created me—God. I have a beauty all my own, unlike anyone else's, so why change it or want to look like someone else? God doesn't make mistakes: I am who I'm meant to be. I'm not perfect, but I am a perfectly imperfect me. We are not all the same; we're uniquely different—different with similarities. I was beginning to finally get it.

I'm different, and it's time I lifted the burden of feeling inadequate off my shoulders. It's too heavy to carry anymore, and I don't have to. I can let a lot of worry go and stop focusing so much on what I look like or don't look like.

With all of the self-doubts I had, no wonder dating was hard for me. If you think something will never happen or be a part of your life, most likely it won't. It's true that, in anything, what you think does play a big part in your success. I may have thought I hid my insecurities well from everyone, but my body language often spoke more than what I said.

I remember how scared and nervous I was when I attended my first LPA event. I didn't know what to expect or how to feel. Should I have felt anything else except excitement about meeting other people who looked like me? I would be able to talk face-to-face and eye-to-eye with others. This was a novel and yet uncomfortable thought. I was used to being in and a part of the average-size world, not the little-people world. These two worlds seemed separate to me. I didn't have little-people friends nearby. I only saw other little people when I went to an LPA event, which didn't happen often enough for me to feel very comfortable. My parents took me to a few, and all I saw was that I didn't look like the others. They looked different.

It wasn't until I got older that I decided on my own it was time to meet other dwarf people similar to me. I wanted to know about their lives and what they thought about themselves. What were their stories about school and dating, some of their hopes and fears, challenges, dreams, and goals? What did they think about not being average height or being around others who were not like themselves? Going to a Little People event scared me, and it was overwhelming, exciting, and fun too. I met a lot of great individuals, and I looked forward to seeing them again. I wasn't able to go as often as I wish I could have, so I didn't always feel comfortable or develop the relationships I had hoped to, but the experiences and people changed my life.

The chapter I belonged to held a bowling event, and I was excited to go, especially since I had my own bowling ball. I liked bowling and went often on my birthdays. And because my short, fat fingers made it hard for me to find a ball I could bowl with, my parents got me my own ball, which I was thrilled to receive. Never again would I have to try to find a ball that was big enough to fit my fingers without being way too heavy.

It had been a long time since I had gone to my first LPA activity. This time I drove and went by myself. I was quite nervous about going into a room where I might not know anyone, so I sat in the car for a while just thinking about it.

Then I thought, *This is crazy. Here I am, in high school, and I'm afraid to go in because of what others will think of me. Oh boy. But they're just like me.* What was I so worried about? *Just because I'm a dwarf like them doesn't mean they are all going to like me. Just like any other time, they need to get to know me, and I, them.* The bigger question I needed to ask myself was, would I let them? Memories flashed through my mind of being made fun of and called all sorts of names, feeling alone and left out in a crowded room. But I was older, so wasn't I past this kind of thinking by now? I guess not quite.

I sat in the car a little longer and then decided this was ridiculous. I hadn't driven all this way to turn around and head back home, so I went in. And there it was again: they looked different than I did. As I saw other little people talking to each other, checking out shoes, searching for the elusive ball, laughing and having a good time with each other, I felt out of place. What did the feeling of knowing I belonged feel like to me, though? I wanted to walk out the door and leave. Did I really look like them? I saw a small part of myself in them, but it wasn't what I saw when I looked in the mirror. They were different, just like everyone else.

Little people come in all different sizes and shapes, with different types of dwarfism and backgrounds. Yet something kept pulling me to stay. *Give it a chance. Give them a chance. Give myself a chance.* It's easy to run away when we aren't comfortable or feel intimated. It takes courage to do things that seem hard and uncomfortable, but it can be incredibly rewarding when we step out of our comfort zones.

When I entered the bowling alley and saw other little people, I didn't get the feeling I was hoping for. Maybe my expectations were too high, thinking everyone would be so excited to have me there that many would automatically come up to me and let me know they were. I'm not sure why I expected that when I had a hard time accepting myself, lacked confidence, worried about what others thought of me, and kept to myself. There was no event or experience, and certainly no one person, that was going to fix how I felt and what I thought about myself—except me.

Looking at the group of little people, I thought, *I am not one of them.* I didn't look like them; I didn't have funny short arms and legs and waddle when I walked. Yet I decided to stay anyway because I needed to stay, even if I was out of my comfort zone. A few of them eventually came up to me and said hi, and we talked for a while. Then I was asked if I wanted to bowl with them, and I said great, that

I would love to join their group. They introduced me to a number of other little people, and I was thrilled.

Since I was the new girl of this group, having them help me meet others made it so much easier to relax and have a good time. They helped me bring my guard down, the wall I had built to protect myself. I ended up having a great time bowling and talking with them. I began to not see the differences we had on the outside; what I ended up seeing were individuals, just like me. We had more similarities beyond being little people.

Meeting this group of little people was the beginning of building a bridge between being in the dwarf community and living in the average-size world. I was inspired by many of them, by the things they did, wanted to do, had accomplished already, and hoped for. I admired them because they didn't seem to let things get in their way like I did—being different, people's laughter or rude, derogatory comments, or discouragement from others. I didn't see that they let all of that crazy stuff get to them like I did. They were thriving and not just surviving in high school and college, in careers and relationships. I was inspired by them because they were just like me, little people.

I left that event inspired by everyone I had met and with a new perspective on life and being a little person. It opened up my eyes to other possibilities. I couldn't wait until the next event because I wanted to hang out more and make lasting friendships. I realized I needed other little people in my everyday life. I was looking for balance between being a dwarf and living in the average-size world, and being a part of the dwarf community helped me do that.

Although initially I had again looked at them and thought I wasn't like them, the experience finally opened my eyes and allowed me to see I was more like them than I thought. What a wonderful thing. Meeting all of them was a big confidence builder for me. Things were going to be okay even with some of the doubts and hang-ups I still clung to and the new challenges I would face.

The Little People of America organization continued to impact my life, personally and professionally. I didn't realize how much of an impact it had until later.

At another gathering there was one little person who I thought was the cutest guy I had ever seen or met. His name was Chris. He was one of those manly men who don't say much but when they do you just crumble because they noticed you. He exuded machoism in a good way. He was very good looking and nice with a quiet demeanor, and I liked him. I really wanted to get to know him, but I didn't think he would notice or like me in that way. He loved sports, dabbled in the entertainment field for a while, and worked in mechanics at one of the auto manufacturing plants. We talked briefly and then went our separate ways. Meeting him was something I knew I wouldn't forget for a long time, even though I probably would never see him again.

Months had passed when I got a call about another Little People event coming up at a friend's house. It was to be a social gathering of friends and other little people to hang out and play games. They wanted to make sure I was included and said they would love to see me there. I was surprised to hear from someone, but excited about seeing and meeting more little people. And I hoped I would see the cute guy again.

A Little Me

When I got there I was glad to see some familiar faces, and then there he was. I was so nervous to go up to him and just saw hi. We were reintroduced and kind of made to talk to each other a little bit. He was definitely popular; everyone knew him and wanted to talk with him as well. I caught myself just staring at him, but when he glanced my way, I quickly turned away. I couldn't let him see that I was interested in him, because I was sure he hadn't given me a second thought.

He was good looking and seemed so at ease with himself, and here I was, so shy and scared. Everyone there was so friendly and seemed so comfortable with each other. They helped me feel that way too, but also made me think, *What am I doing?* Did I take life way too seriously, and had I worried about a whole lot I really didn't have to worry about for so long? I wanted to be confident, like they seemed to be.

A couple of weeks after that event I got a phone call from the cute guy, and he asked me out on a date. He wanted to know if I wanted to go to dinner and see a movie with him sometime. *What?* I couldn't believe it. Suddenly I was on cloud nine. Someone thought I was pretty and interesting enough to ask out? Yep, he did just that. This was going to be my first real date. I didn't know what to say, and I must have paused way too long, because he asked me again. "Well," I awkwardly said, "that would be great, and yes, I would love to."

What do you do or talk about on a date? I felt silly. Wasn't there a social protocol as to what to do and say or not do on a first date? I panicked for a minute when I said yes, and then I just smiled. Wow! A date!

When this man I barely knew picked me up, like most would, my parents wanted to meet him before we went out. I hoped they wouldn't say anything to embarrass me. After clearing that obstacle we drove to the restaurant and then went to see a movie.

The date was exactly how I thought it would be.

We barely said two words to each other at dinner. He wasn't exactly the talkative type as I had thought, and I was scared to death to say anything, so I didn't talk much either. During dinner, he did make the effort to have a conversation, but my responses to him were short and cut-and-dried. Frankly, I felt like a deer in headlights, and for him it was probably like pulling teeth to get me to talk.

Oh boy, I had made it harder than a first date should be for anyone. The poor guy! All I thought about was how everyone had watched us walk into the restaurant and to our table. Then it seemed like people were staring at us. I was used to being stared at when I was by myself, but not with other people, let alone with another little person and on a date. It felt intense and overwhelming. I felt as if I had to be perfect. I wanted to run. Feeling awkward the whole evening, no wonder I didn't say much.

He kept asking me if everything was okay, and it really was, but something got into my head that made me scared of making a mistake. When we went to the movies I felt slightly relieved since we couldn't talk to each other, and on the drive home I felt better with it being just the two of us. But I didn't make the evening easy or as fun as it could have been.

When he dropped me off at my house, I thanked him for a really great time, but deep down I thought, *He's not going to ask me out again.* Although I had behaved terribly on this date, I hoped he didn't think I was terrible.

After he drove off I went in my room and cried. I couldn't believe how I had acted, how I let ridiculous thoughts come into my mind and ruin what could have been a great first date. I didn't say hardly anything, and I probably came across as rude. I was trying too hard to be a "perfect person on a date," instead of just being myself, and ended up being the worst date. I didn't hear from him again.

This was my first and only real date until I got married. I didn't go to prom, and I didn't date in college. A high school dance and one date were the extent of my dating world, so no wonder I didn't think anyone would be interested enough to marry me. As I headed to college, I tried to focus on my education and making lifelong friendships, not on dating. I still hoped one day I would get married and have a family, but for now getting an education in something I wanted to make a career out of had my complete focus.

A new adventure awaited me—being away from home. I was going to leave everything that felt familiar, and that was a little scary. But I was thrilled to be going off to college, far enough away but close enough if I wanted or needed to come home. Going away to college would end up being one of the greatest experiences in my life, and I needed to do this for me. If I didn't, I didn't want to later wish I had. New adventures and experiences were waiting for me to learn and grow from, and I was excited. A new adventure began.

Amy Roloff

Encouragement from Amy:

~It's okay to be afraid and have a little fear. It helps us be discerning about our choices—what we want to do and the people we choose to have around us. It's not okay when we let fear stop us from doing what we want to do and pursuing our dreams. Take that first step, and you may be amazed at what happens next. However, don't let fear—from the littlest to the biggest thing—get in your way, and don't let the what-ifs dictate your life.

CHAPTER 9

Attitude Can Change Everything

A Little Me

One of my favorite TV shows in high school was *The Paper Chase*. That show helped solidify my decision to go to college because it was about friendships, the excitement of learning and accomplishing something tough, the anticipation of going out into the world and making something happen, and everyday student life at one of the most prestigious universities in the country. I fell in love with the university campus depicted on the show, especially in the fall with all its beautiful colors. Based on that show, I had a somewhat romantic outlook on what college life would be like. I did well in high school, and when I received the letter from Central Michigan University stating that I had been accepted, I was very excited.

My first year in college would be one of those woodpecker moments in my life. It would change my life as well as my perception of it.

Arriving on campus the first day reminded me of my first day of first grade. I was excited but also intimidated as we drove to the campus. The closer my parents and I got, the more nervous I felt. *Can we just turn around and go back?* I wanted to stay inside my box, where I felt safe. No. I knew I couldn't turn around. This was going to be such an opportunity for me, educationally and personally.

A new chapter in my life, and it was like starting all over again. I knew I probably wouldn't be called names, bullied, followed home from school, laughed at publicly, intentionally excluded from activities, and so on as I had been in high school, but I would have to embrace how people reacted to me, whether in a positive or negative way, and I would have to make even more of an effort to show myself and everyone else that I belonged here, on this campus. It was my choice to go to college (maybe influenced a little by my favorite TV show).

It was comforting that the college was close enough that I could go home for the weekend if I really wanted to. But it was far enough away that I couldn't run home to my dad all the time so he could come to my rescue. I had to handle whatever came my way myself. I'm glad I didn't turn around and go back home and stay where it felt safe and familiar. I made a bold decision to get out of my comfort zone, and it was the best thing I could have done.

As elated and excited as I felt one moment about this new adventure, while unpacking my things, I then thought, *What was I thinking?* I was so looking forward to attending college that I had built it up as this perfect place and experience, but I didn't get the comforting feeling I thought I'd get when I got to campus and entered my dorm room. I needed to give it a chance.

The university was only a two-and-a-half-hour drive from my home, the only home I'd ever known. My dorm room and the college campus were going to be my new home for a few years, which was a little scary to me, and the realization suddenly hit me: *I'm alone.* Where was my go-to place when I needed to just hide and think and breathe and gather the confidence to get up and say, *You can do this, Amy?* College was a big place, and I didn't know anyone there. I needed a little familiarity to bridge the gap from old and safe to new and scary.

After my parents and I unloaded all of my things, we took a walk around the campus so I would be more familiar with my surroundings. The campus was gorgeous, just as I remembered from orientation—the big maple trees, the older brick buildings scattered around campus, the central walkway that cut through the grounds, the residence halls on the outskirts of campus, old downtown . . . We even found a church I could attend.

I began to think more about the many possibilities that lay before me, ready to launch me into my future, and feelings of insecurity seemed distant at that moment. The lifelong friends I would possibly make, getting an education and a BSBA degree with a major in accounting and a minor in hospitality—thinking of these things made me feel more as though this was going to be okay. *I'm going to make it, and going to college was definitely a good choice.*

Then we drove around town to see more of the area and went out to dinner. Afterward, we came back to the residence hall I would call home for the next year, and some of my excitement about starting college seemed to leave. I didn't want to say goodbye to my parents, but I had to. Then my parents drove off.

As I returned to my dorm room I suddenly felt alone again. There was no one else in the room, though I could see that one of my roommates had moved in already and I had missed meeting her. Even though I had shared a bedroom with my two older sisters most of my life, I enjoyed having a room to myself for a few years. Now I would have roommates, strangers really, that I didn't know. Hopefully, we would all get along with each other.

What happens if they can't handle having a roommate that is different, out of their norm? What if they don't like me? What happens if we don't get along?

My mind went crazy as the what-ifs came back in full swing. I conjured up so many scenarios, what-ifs, mostly of what could go wrong instead of what could go well. I knew I was feeling alone at that moment and letting missing home and what was familiar get to me way too much. I tearfully fell asleep that first night.

I often thought I had something to prove to others and myself over the years, even though I knew I was like everyone else, just physically different. I never seemed to be able to escape the feeling of having to prove myself. It followed me into college, and even to this day to some degree. I hoped I would figure out how to have good conversations and live with four people who were strangers to me. This was just as new to any other first-year college student, but I made it into something big, really big, for myself.

I put a lot of stress on myself that year by trying to be the perfect roommate and by being a people pleaser. As a result, I ended up accruing other health issues related to the surgery I had four years earlier. Not wanting my roommates to know anything about this, I did my best to hide it from them by getting up earlier than they did to deal with it. I didn't want to be a burden or a complicated roommate. However, wanting to be the perfect roommate caused me to feel like a fragile egg, afraid I would crack if I opened up and was vulnerable by sharing my thoughts and feelings.

I think about it now, and, seriously, how can you live with anyone, let alone four other women, and not have personal conversations with them, not share and be vulnerable? Isn't that what most girls do—get personal?

Well, I continued to work hard on trying to be the perfect roommate—cordial, helpful, a part of what was going on in our room and on our floor, listening to them share stories and talk about their dreams and hopes. I wanted them to know I was truly interested in them, while not sharing anything personal myself. This charade, along with hiding the stress I was putting on myself, went on for months until just before Christmas break. This was a pivotal moment that changed how I saw others and myself.

A Little Me

I bought a little Christmas tree and other decorations to decorate our room for the Christmas holiday. My roommates brought other decorations as well, and together we made our room very festive during the few weeks before we left for Christmas break. A few days before we all left to go home, my roommates came to me and said we needed to talk. The way they said "we need to talk" made me very nervous and scared. What was wrong? What did I do? Weren't things going great? But right then everything didn't seem okay. I was trying so hard to be the perfect roommate, so what could it be? All day I could hardly go to my classes and concentrate on my studies because I was distracted by wondering what in the world this roommate talk could be about.

Before we opened the Christmas presents we had gotten one another, each of them expressed that she couldn't handle having me as a roommate anymore if I didn't change. If I didn't find a way to change, then I would need to find other roommates to live with next semester.

What?

This came as a big shock to me. This whole talk was about me. They felt that I was being arrogant, distant, uncommitted, closed off, and unfeeling. They didn't feel comfortable with me anymore because they didn't know how to talk to me. After months of living together, they didn't really know anything about me. I was still a stranger to them.

I was stunned. What was happening? I was devastated, hurt, and so surprised! I had tried so hard to fit in and to be perfect, and thought everything was going okay, except it wasn't, for me or for them. *Where did I go wrong?*

In the end, after listening to them share their thoughts, all I heard was that no matter how much I had tried to be the perfect roommate, to be liked by them, it wasn't enough. All they wanted was to get to know me, and I didn't let them do that. It suddenly dawned on me that it didn't matter to them that I was different, a dwarf. To them I was Amy, their roommate whom they didn't know very much about because I hadn't allowed them to.

I started to cry, partly out of relief because I didn't have to keep trying to be perfect and partly because I didn't know what to do now. Everything I thought I was doing right ended up being the complete opposite; I was doing it all wrong. They were asking me to leave after Christmas break if I didn't or couldn't change. It wasn't about changing who I was but about letting them get to know me. I had to change my mind-set and learn that it's okay to be vulnerable and allow others to know Amy a little more from the inside, not just an image from the outside. I was being given the okay by my roommates to take a chance, that they would be there for me and we'd finish out our freshman year together.

Perhaps that's all I needed—someone reassuring me that it doesn't matter if I'm different. However, I'll always be looked at differently if I keep others from getting to know me, because different is all they see, instead of someone who has feelings, hopes, and dreams, just like them.

I ended up crying more, and then we all started to cry and hug each other. I told them I was so sorry, that it definitely wasn't what I had wanted to happen, for them to feel like I didn't care about them. I didn't want to leave; I would try to be a better roommate, to open up more, share, and be a little more personal. We agreed to give being roommates together another chance. I really did want to have good friendships with all of them. It was an emotional time; it took everything I had to hold myself together, hearing what they were saying to me, and not take it so personally. I was exhausted.

Well, it definitely wasn't how I had imagined my first semester in college. After Christmas break we'd start over. I felt tremendously better after crying together and getting all emotional. It was as if the ice had been broken and we could just be ourselves. I could now let go of the big weight I had placed on my own shoulders. We were able to celebrate Christmas together by opening the presents we had gotten each other and laughing, crying, and eating junk food. It truly ended up being the best college Christmas.

I went home for Christmas break and had time to reflect on what my roommates had said. I thought about my earlier school years and all the time I wasted worrying about stuff I didn't need to worry about, things I had no control over—all the what-ifs and what others thought about me. Then it dawned on me again: being a dwarf was not the problem. The problem was with me and in my mind, what I thought about being a dwarf and what I assumed others thought about it. I never gave anyone a chance to embrace and be okay with my being a dwarf and to get to know me. I had taken that away from them.

Whatever preconceived ideas I had about it and my preoccupation with what others thought about me took a toll on me, and the talk with my roommates woke me up to what I was doing. Being different, a little person, didn't matter to them, and I should never have made it an issue within myself. They just wanted to get to know me. Sure, maybe they were a little surprised when they first met me, but after that I was just a person like anyone else. However, I made it hard for others to get to know me because I didn't let my guard down enough to open up to them. I was afraid. I wanted to have real, honest conversations but was often unwilling to engage in that myself. To my roommates I wasn't a person whom they could relate to because I didn't open up enough to let them get to know me. I thought if I kept the door closed to my inner thoughts and feelings, no one would see my imperfections and have a reason to walk away.

My freshman year in college was a moment that helped me realize I had made being a dwarf so much more of an issue for myself than anyone else really did. Trying to be the perfect person and wanting to please everyone prevented them and myself from finding out who Amy is. I realized I didn't need to try to be perfect all the time—I knew I wasn't ever going to be perfect. It was a classic setup for feeling as if I failed at everything, or at least often. I couldn't live up to the expectations I put on myself, expectations I should never have had. Trying to be perfect, to fit in and be like others, resulted in setting myself up for failure. All I needed to do was just be myself. That would be perfect enough. In order to do that, I had to relearn to really like myself, flaws included, and what was so wonderfully unique about me. My dad would always tell me, "Just be the best of you, Amy. That's all you or anyone can ask for."

To say that the rest of my college years went smoothly and things were great would be an overstatement. But that first year gave me a better outlook and sense of purpose. It helped me realize I needed to value myself first before I could expect others to, as well as understand what my purpose was and go after my dreams. Did I change as time went on? I sure hope I did, for the better. Hopefully, the core of me remained intact. I think it did.

Sometimes we get so wrapped up trying to please others that we end up closing ourselves off and don't realize we're doing it until it's almost too late. We forget about taking time to pursue our goals and dreams instead of watching others do it. I wasn't a little girl anymore, but a young woman trying to figure out life and what I wanted to do with it. I knew education was important because it was one thing no one could take from me. It was an opportunity to pursue what I wanted to do—make a difference in other people's lives.

I then decided to set up the rest of my college years ahead for success. This was about Amy and what I needed to do. I couldn't keep wasting time on what others thought about me or what I should be doing. What a freeing relief when that weight began to lift off my shoulders.

***

My job experience thus far consisted of a part-time job working for a wallpaper company in the summer of my senior year of high school. Then I was off to college. I applied for a number of jobs and felt defeated after being turned down so often because of this or that reason, or because I didn't quite "meet the qualifications." My parents always encouraged me to not throw in the towel and say "poor me."

After my first year in college, I had the opportunity to apply for a desk receptionist job in my dorm. The few campus jobs available were hard to come by because so many people wanted them, but I thought, *Why not? What do I have to lose except getting turned down?* And feeling I already had that experience down, I applied.

The resident hall director had a get-together for all of us who had applied and were now in the second round of interviews, as well as the resident assistants (RAs) and the head desk receptionist. I was surprised when I got a letter stating that I had made it to this interview stage. *Could this really happen?* As I looked around, there were a lot of other candidates I had to beat out for the few available openings. I felt intimidated by all the people there. But I made it this far, so I still had a chance and might as well follow through with it.

I put the brakes on the negative self-doubting talk that was creeping into my mind about not getting the job because I presumed they would think I wasn't good enough or was too short and couldn't handle some of the responsibilities. I went for it anyway.

I was nervous going through the interview process. The hall director had a very direct, in-control, and intimidating personality. This was not going to be an easy process, but if I got through it, it would be an accomplishment. Regardless of the outcome, I was proud of myself for pushing through and not running away. It was a difficult interview with questions about hospitality, how I would handle students from other residence halls who wanted to come into the all-women dorm after hours but weren't allowed, procedures, follow-through, and so on. I was unsure of how I did; it could go either way. I got the news a few days before my freshman year ended, before we all went home for summer break, that I had gotten one of the few desk receptionist positions. I couldn't believe it! I couldn't wait to let my parents know.

Soon after my sophomore year began, my resident hall director told me she was a little uncertain about me at first because of my lack of experience working with the public. She wondered if I could handle the pressure that came along with the position, but she decided to give me a chance anyway because she saw something in me that was worth giving me the opportunity. I appreciated her honesty but even more that she had given me a chance. It's all I needed—a chance. I loved the position, the interaction with everyone in my hall. It led to meeting many people and a few lifelong friendships. My confidence grew, and I felt more capable and encouraged that I could do this. And frankly, I could do most anything if I put my mind to it. It was more than just believing in myself; it was not being afraid of success or failure, or what others thought about me, and learning how to pick myself up.

One of my first confrontations as a desk receptionist for the resident hall I lived in came in my sophomore year, late on a Friday night. The girls' hall was right next to the boys' hall, with a connecting hallway between the two dorms. On this Friday night, it got pretty hairy and scary. There was a lot of activity, with students coming and going in the hall. The doors were locked at midnight sharp, and afterward no one was allowed in the hall except for students who lived there, no exceptions. Often, a guy would come and want to hang out with one of the residents, but we couldn't let him in. He had to call the girl, and she had to come down and let him in.

This night there was a lot of pounding on the door between our two dorms. I went to see what in the world was going on. Several guys wanted to get in the girls' dorm to see a friend. I told them I was sorry, but they couldn't come in unless she came down to get them. They kept pounding on the glass door, and I started to get scared that it would break and they would come barging in anyway and trample over me. I just kept saying no, I could not let them in. They weren't happy about that and used a few vulgar words and rough language.

I'm not sure what got into me, but I stood my ground. I just hoped the glass wouldn't break and the situation wouldn't get worse. Besides, I could call campus police for help if I needed to. My heart was pounding, and all I wanted was to be able to handle and diffuse the situation. I didn't want to lose my job over this.

They kept pounding on the door and yelling some pretty awful things at me, and for the last time I said I couldn't let them in, and then I walked away. I hoped they would just turn around and go away. Guys who had been drinking and were a whole lot bigger and stronger than I was did not want to be told they couldn't do something by a short girl. Thankfully, they eventually left.

Whew! I drew a huge sigh of relief. I was so proud of myself for standing my ground and not being intimidated by such big guys. The glass door between us gave me a little confidence, and I was glad that small barrier held up to their pounding. It got around the dorm that "this stubborn short girl wouldn't let us in. She was tough."

My first two years of college were an eye-opener for me. They changed my perception of myself as well as how I thought others viewed me. Those two years changed me for the better and have impacted my life ever since. I'm not here to say everything went great, but those years gave me a healthier perspective and enabled me to overcome tough challenges in a much more positive way.

It took five years to complete my degree. I decided not to major in accounting because I couldn't see myself doing accounting work all the time and worrying about being off by a penny. So I changed to a double major in what I thought of as the most people-oriented areas of business—human resources and hospitality.

To this day, I still wish I had gone after a degree in education because deep down I really wanted to teach. I should have made that decision to change degrees then, but I thought I was too far into business to change completely. My hope and dream was to open my own restaurant or a bed and breakfast one day.

A Little Me

Although I can't go back and redo any of the choices I made then, I hope I learned from those years. I graduated with a BSBA degree in human resources and hospitality. I have always valued my college years and never regretted going, regardless of what degree I ended up getting or what I ended up doing afterward. I learned so, so much about myself, life, and others, and what an important part my faith had in my success in college.

We've all heard how important our attitude is. It's critical. A positive attitude is powerful. It has the ability to lift us up and not tear us down. It helps shape our character, how we see life and other people, how we face challenges, and when the chips are down, it helps get us back on our feet. Attitude isn't just about verbalizing and puffing up our image and ego with all kinds of self-affirmations to help us feel better about ourselves. It's about being real, honestly digging deep down and believing what we think and say. In success or failure, keep believing and know you are a wonderful person. I'm worth it. I mattered yesterday, I matter today, and I'll still matter tomorrow. And I have a purpose every day. Having a good attitude helped me to understand that it's not about me, but it's better to have a servant heart than boosting up an ego or dwelling on insecurities.

College helped me see how my attitude affected a lot of what I did and how I saw life. So much can affect our attitude, but nothing is harder on ourselves than our own self-image. I didn't always have a great attitude about myself. On one hand, I thought I was pretty darn good, and yet on the other, not so great. Everyone just seemed better than me no matter what I did. But I had hope, and that is powerful too.

The end of my freshman year was a big turnaround for me. It was a wake-up call to stop the internal self-pity. I grew up being taught that having a "poor me" demeanor was not acceptable. We can't build up resilience or move forward with an attitude of self-pity. It was about making changes in myself from the inside out. Life is tough sometimes—so what? It's also wonderful. If I kept focusing on the challenges I had instead of the opportunities to be an overcomer and succeed, then the challenges would seem bigger than they really were. It's not healthy to focus on the outside all the time, hoping the inside will catch up.

It took roommates who wanted to kick me out of our dorm room to wake me up. It took the success of getting a coveted job to give me a little more confidence in my abilities. It was the beginning of seeing that life would have challenges but that I had the ability to take chances and overcome them. It was an opportunity to embrace life instead of pushing it away and hiding from it. It was time to see that life would be full of wonderful, happy, successful, fun moments as well. Each day ahead is an adventure, an opportunity, and I'm excited to see what they will bring.

Encouragement from Amy:

~ We can hope, set goals, have passion, plan, and desire success all we want, but it takes faith, hope, and most definitely some sort of action on our part to make things happen.

CHAPTER 10

One Thing Can
Lead to Another

A Little Me

I had a dream—well, several really: to open my own restaurant; to become a teacher; to do my internship at a hotel or bed and breakfast in one of my favorite places, Mackinac Island; to be a mom one day; to help others be successful in their jobs; and, ultimately, to give back in some way to help others. I'm not sure I believed I would ever truly make a difference in other people's lives.

As I got older and the years passed by, my perspective on life and some of my dreams changed, but I always wanted to help someone else. The what-ifs still played their part, but they showed up once in a while instead of all the time. What-ifs are like weeds: when you think you have destroyed them so they won't come back again, suddenly they find a way to creep back and grow even bigger and more invasive.

After college I realized I needed to get out there and pursue what I wanted. I couldn't just wait around for things to happen. I needed to have the desire, determination, and can-do attitude to go after my dreams. I couldn't depend on others always being around to help me out, or make excuses that my dreams didn't happen because I was different, a dwarf. I needed to go after them by being bold, having a plan, and believing in the goals I wanted to accomplish.

In college I had hoped to complete a double major in hospitality and human resources. I found out this was possible, but I needed to do the required internship in hospitality. However, I didn't expect it to be as hard as it was to get an internship. Once accomplished though, I would leave college with a well-earned degree. I had my work cut out for me. What intimidated me was making lots of phone calls and putting together a résumé—that was a challenge. For one thing, I'd only had one summer job, and that was before I entered college. For another, I needed to sell myself, and I wasn't good at that, but I had to try and do my best because I needed the internship. So, with a lot of faith, prayer, and grit, I got to work.

I sent out a number of résumés to various places, such as hotels big and small, restaurants, and event-planning businesses, in the hope of getting that elusive internship. I was hoping to get an internship anywhere, gain a little on-the-job experience and knowledge, and complete my degree. Who knew?—maybe I would end up working where I did my internship.

I hadn't worked in the hospitality industry before except in my own kitchen, entertaining and cooking for my family and friends. I tried not to think that being different might cause others to see me as incapable of working in the hospitality industry. I didn't know of any other little person that was, but I figured that since I did so much in my home kitchen, this would just be on a bigger scale. I didn't think about actually working in a restaurant kitchen or at the front desk of a hotel, but rather behind the scenes, helping manage the overall business.

I was accustomed to using stools and assumed I would use one in some capacity on the job. Then I wondered, *Would that many stools be allowed in a restaurant kitchen—to reach sinks, counters, the stove, the refrigerator—and would that pass inspection? Would that crowd the kitchen with everyone moving around everywhere? How about a stool at the front desk or in housekeeping or the business offices of a hotel?*

I didn't anticipate there being a problem, because stools were a part of my life, what I needed to accomplish the task at hand. However, when it came to business, that could be a whole different story. I needed to be prepared for the questions that might arise. I worked hard on not feeling like I had to please everyone, but I did need to sell myself, to convince a potential employer that I could do the work, that I was qualified and capable. And I was ready.

I had a friend and mentor, who was also a little person, that heard I was looking for an internship and offered to make some phone calls for me. I was elated when she offered to help, because I had already received a number of rejection letters, saying either they didn't have an internship, they were filled, or a polite "thank you for your interest" but I wasn't qualified enough. I felt a little deflated and discouraged, but I wasn't yet defeated. I still had a little hope left. It wasn't that I wouldn't graduate, I just wouldn't graduate with the double major I had my heart set on.

I reached out to a little-person friend of mine who knew the contact person at a hotel. She came back to me with great news. The hotel had an opening for an internship, and if I was interested, it could be mine. They just needed me to send in my résumé along with a letter and come in for an interview beforehand to get it all set up. So that's just what I immediately did.

After our brief interview and a phone conversation, I would be starting in a week. The hotel was about an hour and a half from my house, so I had to find a place to stay. My friend graciously said I could stay with her and her husband since it was for such a short time and minutes from where I'd be working. I couldn't wait. I was so excited but absolutely nervous and a little overwhelmed as well. Things were really starting to come together, finally.

Then it happened.

Just as I was heading up there, I got a letter saying the internship had been canceled and they didn't have one available for me anymore.

Amy Roloff

What? What happened?

I was upset, even a little angry. How could they do that? I was ready and had my heart and mind so set on it. I talked with my friend, and she agreed that I should go talk with them—they might have something else—and at least find out what had happened. I decided to go because I wanted to know what had happened and what this "something else" might be. I didn't expect anything, but—who knew?—it might be worth the time. I was mad enough that I wanted them to look me in the face and tell me why the internship was suddenly no more.

This wasn't the first time I had been turned down for a job, but it was the first time I felt the need to deal with the situation head-on by meeting with someone face-to-face. I just couldn't believe it or understand it.

I was running out of time to do an internship in order to complete my requirements for a hospitality degree and graduate on time. I felt so close to double majoring in human resources and hospitality, but now it didn't look like I'd be able to do that.

I met with a gentleman at the hotel and watched him squirm a bit while talking with me. There was still no internship available or any other opportunity at the hotel right then. He didn't have an explanation for why I had been told I had the internship and now there wasn't any. Who does that? Even though I expected it, I was still crushed. All I felt like doing was getting out of that place as soon as possible and crying. What more did I need to do or could I do? Maybe nothing.

I did wonder, though, if the reason I didn't get the internship was because I was different. What would the guests think, or how would they react when they saw me, a dwarf, behind the desk or in the marketing office, representing the hotel? I didn't know and would never find out. Maybe it was just that life didn't work out this time. No matter what the reason was, I knew I couldn't dwell on it.

My hope and dream was being whisked away from me, and I didn't know what else to do or what more I could say to advocate for myself and insist they fulfill their written and verbal commitment to me. This was business, not personal, but I didn't like it. This opportunity was my last hope to gain the experience I needed to get a double major. Besides, I really wanted it.

Since it took an extra year to graduate from college when I changed my major, I didn't have the time or financial resources to continue on. College life had to come to an end. So I graduated with a BSBA degree with a major in human resources and a minor in hospitality. And that was a BIG accomplishment, and I was proud of myself! I would gain the experience I needed in the hospitality industry some other way, over time.

I could have crumbled after not getting the internship and viewed it as another setback, letting me go backward, thinking the same old, same old thing—*it's about me being a little person. This dwarf thing is getting in my way. No one is going to believe in me enough to think I can do anything. Why do others seem to feel uncomfortable being around me?* I could have given up, moped around, and gone back to what seemed familiar. *Why not give up and move on to something else?*

I couldn't, not this time. I just couldn't go there again. I didn't want to, and why should I? So what if I didn't get an internship or job? Yeah, it was my dream and passion, and it didn't go the way I pictured it, but it wasn't as if I were the only person to ever be turned down for an internship or a job. It wasn't as though my dream and passion in hospitality had to end. It just might show up as a different kind of opportunity.

I accomplished a goal and dream of mine, and it's still big to me to this day. So, with cap and gown on, I proudly walked across the stage to receive my diploma. I did it! My parents, sisters, brother, and a good friend were in the crowd to watch the pomp and circumstance. I was elated, and my parents were so proud; they knew this had been a hard feat to accomplish. I walked down the steps thinking, *I did this and I'll do a lot more in life. I do matter and have value and a purpose.* I was ready to go out into the world and make something happen in the next chapters of my life.

I learned once again that when life doesn't happen the way we plan and hope for, it's not the time to give up or lose confidence in ourselves; it's the time to pull up your pants and keep forging ahead. It's a time to keep building the community of people you want and need around you personally and professionally. It's the time to take stock of what you need and want to do.

I didn't stop believing in my dreams and pursuing my passions; they were just delayed a little. I didn't want to keep being the kind of person who gives up too easily when life gets tough or doesn't go the way I planned. I did that way too much.

However, it wasn't always easy giving myself positive affirmations, because I sometimes felt I was being self-indulgent in doing that. There were times I wanted to find an easier route when it seemed too difficult. Others are able to forge ahead and keep pursuing their dreams even though it's tough, and I can and should too. If at first I fail, try, try, and try again.

Not getting the internship was a good reminder for me to keep trying. Most things that are difficult are worth pursuing. We need to always think that success is just around the corner. Look what I've accomplished—things I didn't think possible back in my high school and college years. More opportunities will come along, and I want to be ready for them when they do. I built upon my accomplishments and the positive things going on in my life. I was going to keep moving forward, not stay stuck.

Don't dwell on the past or what didn't work out. There will always be possibilities that lie ahead, and I don't want to put the bar so low that I don't give myself due credit, but neither do I want to put it too high. It's good to be challenged, to have the bar just high enough to keep reaching and striving for something. Challenges are to be overcome. It's what builds character, strengthens us, and helps us keep learning and growing. I wanted to be an overcomer, to be able to look back and say, Yeah, *I did it.*

I revamped my résumé and started looking for a job—hopefully, THE job—but if not, then a job that would be a stepping stone toward what I really wanted to do—work in the hospitality industry. I wasn't thinking about my personal life—having a relationship, getting married, or any of that stuff. I had no time for that. My professional life needed to be a priority. One day I hoped I'd get married and have a family. Only time would tell.

After college I went back home for a while. After several months I found a job, and now I had goals, a plan for my future, and I was still open to opportunities that might come my way in the hospitality industry. And I had a loan to pay off. I didn't want to be the person just sitting around at home waiting for someone to call. Before, I would have done that, but not now.

Amy Roloff

I called my friends who were still in the area and invited them to go to the lake or on hikes. I even got the courage to go to some local LPA events. After working for six months, I started to look into finding an apartment and moving out of my parents' house. I was figuring out what being an adult was all about. My college life was finished; I couldn't just sit around and wait for life to happen. I needed to be involved in life, not just watch life go by.

My college years helped me appreciate and enjoy being myself, as a little person. Those years also helped me see others not only as tall or average-size people but also as individuals, friends, and coworkers, like I hoped they saw me—as a person, Amy, and not just as a little person. I didn't have any specific expectations except to lose the fear of worrying what others thought of me. I was happy with me, and that's what mattered most.

Entering adult life, I hoped my need to be liked wouldn't get in my way, that I would think *who cares?* instead of creating internal roadblocks. Always worrying about what others think and being a people pleaser take a lot of work. I wanted, and needed, to put that kind of time and work into my future. I needed to let it go. I began to slowly let down my guard, the walls I had built up to ward off rejection, not being liked, failure, being hurt, and not being good enough or beautiful enough.

I started going to a few local LPA events and activities while in college, but after I graduated I decided to not just toy with it but to make it a part of my life. I didn't know very many people in my area, so of course I felt like a newbie, but that started to change the more involved I became. It was time I was a part of the little-people community, full of great people who accomplished so much. I hoped I would make some lifelong friendships.

A Little Me

Putting ourselves out there is scary, but in the end it's worth it because we'll meet other people who may impact our lives for a lifetime. And if not, there will be another time. I didn't want to keep feeling isolated and disappointed about opportunities I missed, or to look back and think, *I should have done this or that, or lived more and tried more.* Life keeps moving on whether I'm on board or not. So I wanted to be more intentional, involved, to take action and just be the best of me. I couldn't go wrong, right?

I had met a really cute guy years ago at one of my first Little People events, and now, years later, I saw him again at a district conference, and my heart stopped. He was as good looking as I remembered, and I thought it would be great if we could reconnect. But time and life move on, and our lives were different by then. Although we weren't meant to be together, we are still good friends today. I met more people and reconnected with others I had met years earlier. I love being a part of something really special, something that has had such an impact on my life. I think about my first Little People event, when I thought, *I don't look like that,* and now I'm glad I belong to such a wonderful community of individuals just like me.

LPA is where I learned more about myself, my type of dwarfism, met my husband, had an opportunity to play sports with others like myself, and where my life changed forever. I met individuals I looked up to as role models and made some really good friendships. Mostly, it changed how I saw myself in the average-size world around me. Average-size world, little-people world—what difference does it make? I can do almost anything I want to if I put my mind to it, just like anyone else. Why let the minor factor of being a little person get in the way? The organization—really the people who formed the

LPA—helped me see so much more potential in myself. I needed to stop comparing myself with others.

There were many individuals who truly paved the way for the rest of us in the little-people community—in the work force, sports, and so much more.

I never got to play sports as a kid, even though I was competitive and would probably have been good at some sports. But when you see yourself at a disadvantage before you even begin, it's hard to get motivated to get out there and try. It's not easy for many who are different.

The nonprofit organization Dwarf Athletic Association of America (DAAA) was formed in 1985 by a small group of little people from my district who got together with a few others to form an organization so little people could play sports and compete with others similar to themselves. This was a big undertaking, but they were determined to make it happen—not just for themselves but for all of us. They took a chance when they saw an opportunity to make a difference. Because of their determination, they've changed so many lives.

The opportunity to play sports with others who were physically similar was huge to me. Besides, winning at a basketball throw in school or casually playing some sports with friends in the neighborhood wasn't anything like competing in a real sport. Now I had a chance to be a part of something.

My first real experience of playing sports was playing basketball the first year of DAAA. That did it for me. We were just a bunch of individuals in the Detroit area getting together for months, practicing. Some of us had never played sports before, while some had been playing for years. We were of different ages, and not all in our youth.

I loved getting together with my team; they were like a second family to me. I had a great chapter and district to be a part of. Being the same height, we were able to look each other in the eye. It was an unbelievable experience.

The year after it was formed, DAAA held its first National Games in Lansing, Michigan, right in my "backyard." No one knew what the turnout would be or how successful it would be, but it was going to be fantastic, regardless. I couldn't wait to play in the Games and experience what my friends got to experience—competition. I was going to be a part of something big for our community. We practiced every week getting ready for the National Games to be held in conjunction with the annual LPA National Conference. There were teams from Chicago, L.A. (the team to beat), New York, Canada, Texas, and all around the country coming to compete.

The big day was about to happen, and I was excited but oh-so nervous. I hoped by just going out on the court and giving it my all I wouldn't let my team down. Competing would obviously be a different experience than just practicing. The gymnasium was packed with spectators from LPA and reporters from the local news stations, as well as family and friends, including my own. Wow! So many people just to watch a bunch of little people play a game. It was awesome.

The first National Games had basketball, swimming, track and field, bocce ball, weight lifting, and a few other sports. Over the years, more were added, like volleyball, soccer, and badminton. What a sight to see little people playing basketball and volleyball! I loved it. I saw others pushing themselves physically and mentally to win and accomplish a goal. It helped me push myself as well. All I can say is that little people are competitive. Maybe the need we feel to be competitive in life transfers to sports.

Our first game started off fast, and before I knew it, it was over and it happened, it really happened—we actually won our first game! We were so thrilled that we were jumping up and down in excitement. But wait, we had more games to play to get to the championship round; the competition wasn't over yet. Although the second game was tough, we won it as well. We couldn't believe it. Our adrenaline was high. My heart was beating so fast I thought it would jump out of my chest. We were just a game away from the championship game.

No way! Unbelievably, we won the third game too. We suddenly found ourselves in the final game for the basketball championship. It reminded me of the 1980 US Olympic hockey team when, in the beginning, no one thought they would make it to the finals, but they won the gold medal. I can still remember watching that game.

We were up against the L.A. Breakers, who were very good and had more experience playing together. They were the favorites. We were considered the underdogs, but winning three games gave us the confidence that we could really do this. We were just proud to have made it to the championship round. Since this was the first DAAA National Games, the winner would be the first to win the gold medal, setting the precedent for future Games in the years to come. We couldn't believe it. We all were so excited.

Every team was required to have a female player on the court at all times. I liked that rule because it gave women an opportunity to play. Usually we couldn't get enough women to play to form enough teams, so I was glad they set it up this way. We had a couple of women, including myself, on our team, but the majority of the players were men. I think there were just more opportunities for men than women back then in schools and community rec programs. Or maybe it was that men went after it more than women did. The guys on our team were confident we could win. They kept reminding us not to let ourselves be overwhelmed by the Breakers or to let our guard down, to go out there and just play our game.

The final game was about to start. This was the game to win, and we adjusted our roster as the game went on. I was getting tired, but that didn't matter. When I made a basket everyone on the team was thrilled. I can't really explain the feeling I had when that happened. All the weeks and months of practice, getting in shape, and learning to play with my team all came together in this final game. A nail-bit-er, it came down to just a few points before the buzzer went off. All it took were two baskets, and WE WON! We really did it! It was absolutely thrilling and one of the best experiences in my life. During the medal ceremony, it was like being at the Olympics. We were the underdogs, but our team won. We got the gold medal at the first DAAA National Games. This was a defining moment that would affect my life for a long, long time.

Unbeknownst to me, there was a guy in the stands who was intently watching me and inquired about me. At the time, however, I was interested in someone else. I would never have dreamed this would be the man I would marry one day.

Playing DAAA sports was a lifelong learning experience I have never forgotten. DAAA changed my life. Sports changed my life. Playing a game, being on a team, and the joys of winning and losing were new to me. Sports gave me the confidence I never knew I had, and it gave me a bigger inner voice to tell myself, *Yes, I can, I'm capable, and don't quit.* It helped me to know that, even when we do our best, our best doesn't always win. But if we don't try, then we've already lost. It's all about getting back in the game. And sometimes when we do our best, we do win.

From the many people I met and the friendships I made, I saw more possibilities for myself as a little person, instead of the limitations I often thought others saw or that I placed on myself. We just do things a little differently than others, and that's okay.

I think sports is a perfect metaphor for life. Playing sports helped me be more disciplined, not only physically but also mentally. Sports helped me push myself and keep going even when I wanted to give up. It helped me better understand that it's not always about me but about others and being on a team, working together for a common goal, giving it our all to win, and having a good attitude and character, win or lose. It helped me realize again that my potential is only limited by my thinking and attitude. When I face failure, I have a choice to make in how I deal with it. The glass can be half full or half empty, and I hope I always choose positivity. Playing sports also gave me the opportunity to experience how success felt and how to be appreciative of it and not abuse it.

Even though we may not always know what the outcome will be, it's worth the effort. If we make rash decisions and quit too soon because something is difficult, we may miss opportunities. Maybe a different outcome is better than we thought. Sometimes I need to be pushed, even if that means to the edge, and to take on some risks. I learned not to run from those times so often, because that's when character and faith are strengthened, and I believe in myself more instead of having doubt. I become stronger. I can do much more than I originally thought.

LPA and DAAA helped me appreciate life as a little person. Just as important was embracing living in what I call the average-size world. It changed how I perceived life, and absolutely for the better.

Don't take life too seriously, and be sure to enjoy the small moments. This experience would help me navigate making a life-changing decision, a big move, and letting some past thoughts go. There were many more life moments and experiences ahead, and I was looking forward to seeing what happened next in my life.

Encouragement from Amy:

~ Taking care of our physical, mental, and emotional health is important, so don't neglect taking time to take care of *all* of you. If you don't, you won't be able to adequately do all that you are capable of doing. You are important, so take care of yourself.

CHAPTER 11

*Little or Big,
It Doesn't Matter*

The question I've been asked most often over the years is, have you ever wished to be average height?

As I think back over the years on how I felt about being a little person, I can honestly say I've never wished I were tall, or an average-height person. The challenges I faced either came from my own doing or just everyday life. They did have an impact on me, and I allowed those challenges to affect my confidence, my self-image, and I put up roadblocks to pursuing some of my dreams and opportunities. But that is in the past, and I try to continue to learn and grow from the choices I've made and from my experiences, to keep pushing forward, excited about what life has in store for me as it unfolds. I can honestly say I just want to feel comfortable with who I am, just being little me in an average-size world.

I've mentioned my faith several times and what an important role it has had, and always will have, in my life because I really want everyone to know it's everything to me. It's the *why* in my life. It's the core of who I am, and my foundation. I've been able to overcome so much because of it, and I'm reminded that I didn't do anything on my own. It has helped me get through some tough moments and challenges that I didn't think I'd make it through. I'm reminded all the time that to God I do matter and have value and a purpose.

A big chapter in my life ended when I graduated from college, and with the opportunity to write the next new chapter before me, I didn't want to rewrite the same old chapters I had just lived. I wanted and needed my future to be different. I didn't want to drag my past into the present and live the same old story—the need to be a people pleaser, letting other people's opinions matter more than my own (it wasn't about seeking advice or having a mentor or a trusted friend to talk to), and thinking I was always less than and never quite good enough. I was tired of that.

I am what I think I am, and I have the ability to define how others see and react to me. It's up to me to change my attitude and thinking—not only how I see myself but also how I see the world and my place in it every day. No one else can do that for me. I know I can count on my faith and God's purpose for me, and trust others in my life to help me stay grounded and not get so distracted by what's not important. I know I've allowed certain situations and other people's opinions to influence my direction and thinking at times because I didn't have enough confidence to stand up for myself and say, *No, this isn't what I should be doing, but yes, this is what I want to do, should do, and I would appreciate your support.*

Whenever I allowed other people's opinions and thoughts to dictate my life, these were some of my weakest moments, which I'm not proud of because I didn't have confidence in myself and I chose not to rely on my faith. I need to believe in and have more confidence and trust in myself. I'm capable of doing more, and I have the courage to do so. Life is risky, but I'm a smart woman. Why not take a chance to see what happens, because so what if it doesn't work out? Not all is lost if it doesn't. The important thing is taking risks and believing I can succeed.

Now, *that* is an important option to consider—believing that, by the choices I make, I will succeed. It's good to remind myself that the glass is half full, not half empty. Things are usually not as bad as we make them out to be; there is always something positive and hopeful we can find. Whether it's personal or business, a positive outlook goes a long way. Negative thinking keeps you stuck, and it's a place I never want to be in—who does? I'm realistic, though, and there is nothing wrong with that. I like to know my choices, along with their pros and cons. I think that is smarter than just taking risks and seeing what happens. It may take some of the thrill and adventure out of some situations, but the important things to consider in life deserve to have some time and thought put into them.

So back to the question that is often asked of me—have I ever wished to be average height? I can honestly say no. I may have looked on the other side of the white picket fence too much, but it wasn't because I wanted to be tall. I was just trying to figure out how to be the best I can in an average-size world. I wish I had used being different to my advantage instead of shying away from it.

I'm thankful for the home I grew up in and for my family that taught me so much. I knew they would always be in my corner rooting for me. I am thankful for the hard work I did and the accomplishment of graduating from college. I'm thankful I became more involved in and a part of the little-people community. These moments, and many more, were some of the stepping stones I needed to push me into adult life.

I may not have gone to my senior prom, that coveted high school tradition, but later I had another opportunity to go to a dance that felt very much like the prom. Attending my first Little People of America National Conference, held in Dearborn in my home state of Michigan, changed my life forever. Not only did I play in the first DAAA National Games, but I attended the big dance the night before the conference ended, which felt like the prom I never got to go to and which I will never forget.

Back then everyone dressed up in fancy dresses and nice suits or tuxes. I was excited to go shopping for the dress I would wear to this dance. And, of course, I chose one I could twirl in, a light-pink satin dress that came off the shoulders, with a lacy floral pattern over it and a hoop skirt underneath. It was so lovely to see everyone all dressed up.

The room was decorated like a formal banquet, with shimmery tables, flowers, corsages available to purchase, cocktails, a red-carpet affair, a mural of Detroit serving as a photo backdrop, a live band and disco ball, and of course scrumptious food. I felt like Cinderella finally getting to go to the ball. I was excited and felt beautiful.

I love to dance, and what an experience to be able to dance with others face-to-face and eye-to-eye. So many were just as tall as or only a little taller than me, and I had hoped one of the two guys I liked would ask me to the dance. My hopes were dashed when neither of them did. As sad as I may have felt at the time, I was still so happy to be there with friends, old and new, and to have been asked by a friend of mine to go with him.

Since this was my first National Conference, I was the new girl, and many people didn't know who I was. And just like in high school or at any other adult function I've been to, we all had a tendency to hang with those we already knew. My first National Conference was my opportunity to get to know as many other little people as I could. Since we came from all over the country, we never knew when we would see each other again. I was just like everyone else there, so it wasn't like going most places where I'm looked at all the time. Regardless of how we looked on the outside and the differences in our physical appearance, we were all similar, and we wanted to be a part of the dance.

I had a blast at my first conference and was sad when it ended much too soon. It was a bold and gutsy move for me to go to a conference where I didn't know anyone but a few from my local area. What memories I still have from it, over thirty-two years later! We didn't have cell phones, email, or social media back then, so I hoped I would be able to keep in contact with many of those I had met by calling or writing letters to them.

I know it may not seem like much, but having felt as though I had to put on a front for so long—only letting people know me from the outside—being vulnerable and letting people get to know me from the inside, personally, was a big risk for me. I was glad I had eventually learned how to reach out to others first, instead of waiting around for them to come to me. I learned to have more boldness, gained confidence, and felt better about myself when I changed my attitude. My attitude about myself had to change before anything else could truly change within me. In turn, I began to see and feel so much better about who I was, what I was, and about my life in general. And seriously, my life really was good back then; I just didn't see it at the time. I hoped it was going to be a whole lot better now.

I kept in contact with many of the people I met at the conference, though it was easy to lose touch since we didn't see each other often, or again unless we went to an LPA Conference, which was difficult because of the expense of attending. Yes, we tried to keep in contact, but that took effort to do so.

There was one particular guy I met who I thought was very good looking, interesting, and full of life. He had done so much more than I had, and I was intrigued by him. He definitely got my attention. I wanted to get to know him better. His name was Matt, and he lived in California. Though he wasn't the one I danced or talked with, he was the one who kept watching me during the conference and when I was playing basketball in the DAAA Games.

Since I had never dated, I had no idea how this would all work out. I didn't want to get hurt—who does?—and being vulnerable was hard. However, I knew I needed to let my guard down, at least a little bit. I tried to contact Matt, but he didn't reply back the few times I reached out to him. So I thought, *I'm not going to waste my time if he's not interested.* I wrote one last time, planning to just let it go if I received no response. Sometimes you meet people and it goes nowhere. Well, he came through in the nick of time and called me, and we ended up talking for hours.

I remember telling myself if I met and did have a relationship with someone, from LPA or anyone else, I wasn't going to let distance be an issue, because most likely the person would not be from Michigan. Distance wasn't going to be a big factor for me in whether a relationship was worth pursuing or not, because a relationship shouldn't be dependent on location. The move for either one of us would probably be based on our jobs, income, and livability. The other question I get asked a lot, and that I asked myself, was, Does it matter whether the person I'm in a relationship with is a little person or average height? No, it does not. What mattered more to me was, *What kind of relationship do I want to have and what am I willing to give to it?*

I remember telling my kids, when they were in relationships, to know and be comfortable with themselves. Someone else should complement your life but not make your life. I wanted them to ask themselves, *What am I looking for in a relationship? What am I willing to give to a relationship? What are my expectations, and what are my boundaries—the line that would be hard to cross or compromise on?*

I gave them an example of two circles: When you're single all you really think about is yourself. However, when you're in a relationship there is someone else you need to consider. It's not about just you anymore. You're a circle and the other person is a circle, and the question is, how are the two circles going to intersect? If the two circles intersect only a little, then the relationship probably won't last long because you're still thinking about yourself more than you're thinking about the other person and your lives together. If the two circles completely intersect, the relationship has a better chance in the long run because you are giving more of yourself to the other than you are taking, and vice versa. You came into the relationship as an individual, and now you are together as a team. It doesn't mean you need to lose yourself completely as an individual, but now you are two individuals coming together as one.

Several months after the conference, Matt and I started a long-distance relationship. We talked almost every day about a lot of things. He worked late, all hours of the day really, and I called him when I got off work. Then, after several months, we began talking about visiting each other. I think we both wanted to see where this relationship was heading. I agreed to go out and see him first. I felt like he was worth taking the chance on. Besides, getting to know someone on the phone is a lot different than getting to know him in person. I wondered if we could actually carry on a conversation face-to-face. I remembered my first date when I barely said a few words to my date. I put some of my worries and what-ifs aside and did what I wanted to do. I didn't want to let distance be the only reason to not get to know someone or have a relationship with him.

I went out in March to see Matt. I had agreed to visit him in a roundabout way. I told him I was also going to visit a girlfriend of mine who was stationed near him. I thought if it didn't work out with Matt, I'd stay longer with my friend. Well, I had such a great time with him that I ended up not seeing her at all, which I felt bad about because my friendship with her was important too. But after talking with her, she told me to go for it and wanted to hear all about it later.

Matt and I had a great visit; he definitely knew how to show a girl a good time. It was a whirlwind. We went to the District 12 LPA conference (District 12 consists of California, Nevada, and Hawaii) being held in Los Angeles. A lot of people remembered me from the National Conference and were surprised to see me in L.A. eight months later with Matt. We had a good time seeing old and new friends.

Matt also took me to lunch to meet his mom, sister, and grand-mother. *What?* He wanted me to meet the three most important women in his life? It happened so fast I didn't have time to think about what that could mean, if anything. It was just a lunch, right? Although I didn't want to make a big deal out of it, I wanted to make a great impression on them too.

After that long weekend, we drove back to the Bay Area. The next day, he took me to Napa Valley, wine country. It was beautiful, and we had a good time. Then I met more of his friends, saw where he worked, and he showed me all around the San Francisco Bay area. What a beautiful city, and what a great experience to see it through the eyes of someone who grew up there—what a trip!

From that trip I realized Matt didn't do anything small. My heart just sang. I was definitely falling for this guy now. We had such a great time, and I hoped it wouldn't be the last. I wanted to see him again soon. Was it love? Yep, it was definitely the beginning for me.

A Little Me

After seeing each other in March, we continued to talk on the phone almost every day. We both wondered where this was going.

Then in April he came to see me in Michigan. I was happy he wanted to see where I lived and meet my family. I was so nervous because I wondered if he would still be interested in me after he left. He met my parents, some of my friends, and I showed him around my neighborhood and told him stories about me growing up. My parents were a little more formal than his, but they were very gracious and happy to meet the person who seemed to be interested in me and had captured their daughter's heart.

I guess visiting me in my home area didn't scare Matt away, for we continued to talk every day for hours after that. I figured it would've been hard to continue that kind of conversation with someone over the phone, let alone in person, if we weren't pretty convinced we wanted this relationship to go somewhere. We both seemed to be on the same page, and we got along splendidly. Yeah, I was falling in love with Matt and told him so.

Then in May I went out to see him again, using up all of my vacation time from work to do it. I didn't care. Although I thought I might know where our relationship was going, I still wasn't sure. I went for it anyway because I really liked Matt and saw the possibility of the two of us being together for life. I just felt it. My heart felt it. I may not have dated anyone else more than once, but with Matt it was different. I was falling in love. It felt real, exciting, comfortable, like a friendship, and we shared the same faith too. That was important to me.

We had another great time, and I dreaded leaving him again. It truly felt like a vacation. He took me to one of his favorite places, Yosemite National Park. I remembered going there on a family camping trip when I was younger, and it was as spectacular then as it was now seeing it with him. We stayed at a nice little lodge near the park and drove all over seeing the highlights of the park, like Half Dome, Glacier Point, and some of the beautiful falls cascading over the mountains.

While at the park, he took me to an overlook that truly showed the majestic beauty of the mountains and the valley of Yosemite Park. I had gone to the rail barrier at the edge to get a better view when Matt called me over to him. He was sitting on a rock ledge behind me. From the way his voice sounded, I knew whatever he wanted to talk with me about was serious. I had no idea what it could be. My heart started to beat faster. I was suddenly nervous. He looked white as a ghost, and I thought maybe something was wrong. I knew he was afraid of heights, so was he feeling sick? Far from it.

I can't remember all he said to me; all I remember is him asking me to marry him.

What? He just asked me to marry him?

I was so surprised, excited, and happy that I started to cry. I said yes! Yes! I suddenly looked at him and realized he was very nervous too. I think Matt was as surprised at himself, that he got up enough courage to ask. We had only been together in person three times before he proposed to me on this fourth visit, but it felt so right, so good. I wanted to shout to everyone that Matt had asked me to marry him and I said yes. I couldn't wait to tell my family and friends. I was so excited about being in love with this man.

The ring he gave me had been his grandmother's and was given to him for the woman he would marry one day. It was the most beautiful vintage ring I ever saw. I loved it. I was overwhelmed and speechless.

Matt asking me to marry him was so unexpected, and yet when he did, the timing was perfect. As we hugged each other, I was filled with happiness at the thought of marrying him.

We came down from the rock, hiked back to our car, and found a phone to call my parents. I wanted to tell them right away. They were very surprised but happy for us as well. I knew they thought this was going a little fast, considering Matt and I had not really known each other that long. But I couldn't imagine life now without him. I knew Matt and I had two very different personalities, but I thought they complemented each other. And besides, I was in love and had just said yes to one of the most important decisions I would make in my life—marriage.

Encouragement from Amy:

~A relationship is about two individuals. Before you get into one, figure out what you want out of it, but more importantly what you are willing to put into it. It's not fifty-fifty or just half of yourself. Both need to give a hundred percent of themselves all the time. You are an individual, so don't lose that, but it's not just about you anymore. It's about giving more of yourself to a relationship.

CHAPTER 12

Big Life Decisions

A Little Me

What did I just do?

I had just changed the rest of my life by saying yes to marrying Matt. We had only visited each other four times in person and talked every day on the phone for about four months. But this wasn't just anyone, this was Matt Roloff, a guy I first met at an LPA National Conference in my home state ten months ago, fell in love with, and said yes to marrying. I know that doesn't seem like enough time to really get to know one another, but it was for us.

The first time I visited him in California, in March of 1987, was the best week of my life. Being with each other and doing so much together solidified everything I thought about him. When the time came to go back home I knew I had fallen in love with Matt. That visit changed my life—I had no doubt that I was in love with Matt; I just wasn't sure if he was with me. Matt's personality was bold and full of life. He was a risk-taker, and life would not be dull with him. It would be a fast-paced whirlwind, filled with excitement. We were different in that sense, yet it still felt right.

Something that did surprise me was how confident I suddenly felt about us being together. I was ready to just up and move away from everything I knew—my home, my family, my church, my friends, my neighborhood and community, my work, and everything else that had been my life—when I said yes. Love and marriage were the beginning of a lifelong relationship and commitment with Matt, and it was worth it to leave everything I had known all of my life for him. I followed my heart in faith for love. I was excited to go on this new adventure with him.

So I moved to California, to a new place to live, new friendships, new work, and everything else that came with beginning a new life and marriage with someone. I was glad I thought beforehand about not letting location be a deciding factor in a relationship. A house can be anywhere because home is always where you are together. I knew I would miss Michigan and my family and friends, but I also knew my family and close friends would always be there for me. My heart is my home, and my home was with Matt. I didn't want to think about the what-ifs or start worrying about the changes that were going on in my life. A few of my what-ifs were, Where would we live, and what kind of job would I get? Would we find a church we both liked? And how often would I be able to come home to Michigan to visit?

As long as we kept our faith, loved each other, and kept communicating with each other, I believed everything would work out. I thought we knew each other well enough to take the leap into marriage and a lifelong adventure together. I didn't think we were rushing into this new relationship too fast. I'm not saying we knew everything about each other, but we knew enough. We would have a whole lifetime of getting to know each other through the experiences we would share. We figured we had enough of a foundation in our similar beliefs and goals in life to take this journey together.

Moving away was still hard for me, though. Michigan and the house I grew up in were the only home I had ever known, my comfort zone. Now I was going to make a new home, totally out of my comfort zone, but I'd be with someone I loved. I wouldn't be alone. Thinking about moving and beginning a new life was exciting. When the time came to actually move, my memory of moving into my dorm room in my freshman year of college came back to me. This time I was moving to an area where I knew at least someone: Matt. I had no job and felt very dependent on him for everything.

But it worked. I was happy. We were different from each other but had enough similarities to keep us together, and we knew we would have a good life together.

We were going to get married. But when and how put us on different pages. He would have liked to have gotten married as soon as possible, and I knew it would take a few months to plan a wedding. It should have given me a clue about how life with Matt was going to be—things would happen quickly (why wait?), and instead of avoiding challenges, his policy was to create our own and take risks in favor of more opportunities. It was a hectic life those first ten years. I tried to keep up as best I could and keep life balanced at the same time.

I planned my wedding in three months. It would have taken four, if Matt could have waited that long. But because he couldn't, I moved it up from October to September. Fall is my favorite season, and I wanted to get married when the leaves were just changing colors.

As I planned our wedding, Matt suggested that we could save time and money if we just eloped. I wasn't sure if Matt was serious or not, but he kept pushing the idea. He would say, "Wouldn't it be cool to elope and then have a less-formal wedding and surprise everyone that comes with 'We're already married'?"

Oh no! No way!

I wanted to have the whole shebang of a beautiful wedding day like I had always dreamed about. Doesn't every girl dream about her wedding day? What kind of dress she will wear, the flowers, the music, and everything else that comes with planning a wedding. I stood firm and insisted, when he kept asking me to elope, that, no, we're having a wedding because this will be our one-and-only wedding and marriage. We went back and forth several times, but eventually I won. Whew!

On a beautiful, warm fall day in September 1987, we got married in the church I grew up in, with family and many of my friends there to celebrate with us. I was never happier than on this day. We had the wedding and reception I had hoped for, and of course I thought this was so much better than having eloped and surprising everyone by already being married. Our wedding day would be memorable for a lifetime to me. So many of my family, close friends, LPA friends, and people I had worked with attended our wedding. It was a dream come true for me.

Matt and I headed to California the next day, where we followed up with a reception with the rest of his family and friends. To me, our entire wedding celebration was wonderfully beautiful and exciting. After the reception, Matt whisked me off in a limousine to stay at the hotel where we first met, and then we flew out the next day for our honeymoon. We stayed a few days in Carmel and Yosemite National Park, where he had proposed. It was such a lovely, romantic time. I was so happy and in love with this guy.

Planning the wedding definitely gave me a hint of how persistent Matt could be when he felt strongly about something. I figured I'd have more of a challenge keeping up with him than he would keeping up with me. I was the one in a new state, new community, new home, and having to make new friends. Everything Matt planned for or wanted to do sounded good to me as I started a new life with him. It didn't seem that Matt's life changed much, except having popped the big question and now living with someone. The months of wedding planning had gone by so fast that I hadn't had much time to think about the personal changes going on in my life. The changes were exciting to think about then, but now reality was setting in. A little change in life is good, though.

Matt helped me settle in and get to know the area. He was a go-getter, the man in charge, and he didn't seem to be afraid of anything. I was quieter, a thinker and a dreamer, and although I wasn't much of a risk-taker, I was up for anything. I loved being around people but didn't like to have a lot of attention drawn to myself. Of course married life changed both of our lives forever, more than we probably thought it would. I know it did for me.

I soon had to get used to the fact that Matt changed jobs frequently—a number of times the first year or two after we were married. Coming from Michigan, the auto capital of the country, I wasn't used to someone changing jobs so often. When we got married, he left a company he had worked at for four years, knowing he wouldn't be able to work the hours he did there and also have a good marriage. Matt's career as a software developer in Silicon Valley was definitely a different environment for me. The companies in the Valley were more project driven, and projects could last from several months to several years. It was a little intimidating to think that Matt could be changing jobs a lot. It didn't seem to bother him; in fact, he seemed to thrive on it.

We moved into his townhouse when we first got married, then bought a brand-new single-level two-bedroom house along the foothills of San Jose about a year later. I had never lived on my own or had a place of my own. I was so excited about getting our first new house together. I loved that little house.

I decided to work at a temp agency for a while to get to know the businesses in the area and think about where I wanted to work and what I wanted to do. After working at a variety of businesses in a number of different positions for several months, I felt fortunate to eventually land a position at Hewlett Packard. I felt good about the opportunities I would have there. Now that we felt a little more settled in our relationship and had found a house, we began to think about starting a family.

My hope had always been to be a mom one day. After trying for some time to get pregnant, I soon found out it would be harder than I thought. We saw a fertility specialist to talk about our options. It was not easy for me to face the possibility of having fertility issues or to even think I might not be able to have kids of my own. I didn't know what else to do.

I would often cry at night and ask God why. I wasn't prepared to face this challenge life had given us. I prayed that somehow my body would be restored and I'd be able to get pregnant on my own without assistance from fertility drugs. I rested on my faith, and regardless of what happened, I knew God always had a better plan and purpose for me. He wouldn't give me more than I could handle, because he's always with me, giving me his strength to help me through whatever I may be facing.

I didn't want to believe this was happening to me, but it was. We didn't know why I was having a difficult time getting pregnant. Was it being a little person that made it harder, or was it because of my illness in my teenage years and all the medication I had been on? Or maybe there was no specific reason. Maybe it just was. I don't re-member the doctor giving us a specific reason as to why we couldn't conceive. We just knew we were going to need help if we wanted to have children. Being two individuals with different types of dwarf-ism was ruled out as a cause, and most likely it wasn't because of my illness either. It was just something we had to face, and we were going to do our best to face it together no matter what the final outcome. We didn't have a choice, really. I had hoped I was done dealing with medications, hospitals, and doctors, but I wasn't.

I wasn't going to let this defeat us. We had both dealt with medical issues before and knew we would get through this too. We had our faith, family, and friends around us. I think dealing with this tough personal challenge together made our marriage stronger.

Matt and I knew the percentages for our having a dwarf baby or an average-size baby, and it didn't make a difference to us either way. Since Matt and I had two different types of dwarfism, our chances of having an average-size baby or a dwarf baby like myself were fifty-fifty. We were very much okay with that ahead of time because, even though I had challenges being a little person and being different and Matt had his own experiences as well, we felt we had come through them pretty well. We had loving parents who had encouraged and supported us our whole lives, and we thought that since we had come out okay, we would be good parents to either a dwarf baby or an average-size baby, having our parents as examples in our lives.

However, over time, the stress that came along with having to go through infertility became hard on our marriage and on me at times. It's not that we fought, but we kept our thoughts and fears to ourselves too much. We were always thinking about it and worrying about it: the timing of everything—*when is the best time to try?*—taking the shots, jotting down everything we did every day, the toll it might have on my body. Trying to have children almost became more business than personal. It took away some of the joy in it all. I didn't really have anyone to talk to about all of this, so I often felt alone as a woman. I didn't know anyone who had gone through fertility treatments. My family was back in Michigan, and it was hard to talk to my sister or my mom because they weren't here.

One thing I hoped I would not face as a result of taking fertility drugs was getting pregnant with multiple babies, like triplets or more. Although I thought my body would be able to bear having twins, I really didn't think it could handle having more than twins. I prayed constantly that I wouldn't have to face making a decision about my health versus the baby's health, or have to choose which eggs to keep and which ones would not survive. Emotionally and physically, I did not want to face those decisions and hoped my faith would not be tested in such a way. I prayed so hard and so often to God to keep that from happening. I kept my fears and worry to myself, and hoped and prayed everything would be okay, that what we had decided to do was the right thing. I was hopeful, very scared, sad, and excited all at the same time.

In the meantime, life seemed to go on as normal. We were getting settled into our little world with our work and new home, and had made some friends through Matt's work and a few from church. I was beginning to feel like I was making our house into a home for us both. Since everything else seemed to be settling down in our lives, I hoped we would be better able to handle going through fertility treatments.

Well, being settled didn't last very long.

After several months of treatment, we finally got the news that I was pregnant. I was thrilled and wanted to tell everyone, but knew it was best that Matt and I kept it to ourselves for a while. I was pregnant with not just one baby but with two. We were going to have twins! My prayers were answered! I was going to be a mom. I couldn't believe it. I was so happy I cried. Four months into my pregnancy, an ultrasound revealed that we were going to have twin boys; one of them would be an average-height baby, and the other would be a dwarf baby.

I loved being pregnant. I wanted to remember every moment just in case these were the only two children I was able to have. Yeah, I got big. I got so big that it looked like my little legs were just poking out from my belly, and I would waddle, like weeble-wobble (but I didn't fall down). I often laughed at myself when I looked in the mirror, but I always had a smile on my face. A lot of everyday things got harder to do. I couldn't tie my shoes or drive a car, and I could barely step on a stool to reach anything because my belly was so big that it got in the way. It was hard for me to cook, and I missed it. I loved cooking and making dinner every night. But I had to make a small sacrifice while I was pregnant and have frozen dinners.

What I looked like didn't matter to me, and I didn't worry about gaining weight. I was just ever so thankful to be experiencing this miracle of life. Yet deep down I had doubts. *Can I handle this? Am I strong enough and physically capable of raising two kids at the same time?* I suddenly felt as if I didn't know anything about being a mom, let alone raising an achondroplastic dwarf, even though I was one, and an average-size baby. They were simultaneously two different worlds.

Although I'm a dwarf, I wasn't jumping up and down with joy wanting a child with dwarfism. I knew it would come with challenges, possible health issues, bullying, and sometimes a lack of opportunities for him, and I didn't want to see my child go through that. So I focused on how blessed I was to be pregnant, to give birth and be a mom.

Amy Roloff

Over the years many people have asked me why I wanted to have kids if I knew they would have the chance of being a dwarf. Why did I want to bring children into the world if they might have so many health issues and life would be harder for them? Wasn't life hard enough, let alone when you are different? I was always so shocked to be approached with those questions. Did they forget who they were talking to—a dwarf woman? Why would anyone ask me that? I got tired of those types of questions in the early years before the babies were born, and even afterward. However, I thought long and hard about those questions.

When I was alone, I did wonder about going through infertility, if maybe I wasn't meant to be a mom. And if so, what was I doing? Maybe I was taking something into my own hands when I wasn't supposed to. My life may not have always been easy, but it definitely wasn't always difficult, sad, or lonely either. I had a good life. I always knew deep down that I was loved. I could do most anything anyone else could do, and I had a lot of fun. Life is always a gift, no matter what. It doesn't matter what you look like or what you can or cannot do. Everyone has challenges, though some have more than others, but still, we each have our own unique life. I believe each life matters, has value and a purpose, regardless.

I know that most of the time those questions were asked innocently enough, but sometimes they hit home hard for me. I think back once again to what my father always told me when I was young: God doesn't make mistakes. God is the one who decides the value of life, not us, even though we try very hard to put parameters around it. God already values and loves each one of us, and he doesn't see us like we see each other. He sees us in his perfect image.

No, God gave me a gift, the gift of becoming a mom, and I was going to do everything I could to raise my boys the best way I knew how.

There were a few people in my life who were a little nervous and worried about whether I would be able to carry twins or not—including my parents. It can be difficult for an average-size person, let alone a little person, to have a multiple birth. I believed with my whole heart that I wasn't meant to go down this road for nothing, and besides, *Why wouldn't I be able to? I can already do most anything anyone else can do, so why not this. I may do things differently, but I can do it.* I did everything I could to make sure these babies came out healthy.

As we celebrated this news, I began to hunker down at work and plan for the arrival of twin boys. Then Matt came to me and said he had a job opportunity in Oregon and we should think about moving.

What?

It had only been two and a half years since we got married and I moved from Michigan to live in California. I was just getting settled in our home. *Now moving again?* I had never moved in my life until I got married. After talking about it, we felt that raising a family in Oregon might afford us more opportunities and allow me the choice of whether I wanted to work or stay at home and raise the kids. This was another tough decision. Matt's work was closely tied to Silicon Valley. Would there be enough work in Oregon if he had to change jobs often? I knew change happens, but I didn't like this change much—it was a big one, and I wasn't quite sure about it.

Matt went to interview for the position just outside of the Portland, Oregon, area. While there, he checked out the area and neighborhoods. He was amazed at the availability of land and the cost of homes compared to in California. There was so much green everywhere, with countryside close to the neighborhoods and downtown Portland, and less traffic. When he got back, he was excited and ready to pack up right away and move to Oregon.

Whoa. I'm six months pregnant. How are we going to do that? My doctor and hospital are here; we have our home, our work, friends and family . . . I'm high risk, and the move may not be good. I'm just starting to get settled.

I knew he was excited about this opportunity, and it would be an adventure for him. He thought he could do so much more for our family and his career if we moved.

He got a second interview, and I flew out with him to check it out. It was a cold, cloudy, rainy January day. I met his potential boss and saw where he might be working. Then we checked out neighborhoods, the surrounding area, hospitals, and a doctor. It was very different than California and reminded me so much of Michigan. *Hmm . . .* I would like the change of seasons here.

Before Matt accepted the position, I had a doctor appointment to see about getting the go-ahead to fly and move at this time, being six months pregnant with twins. Yes, it would be fine, but if we waited a few more weeks, even a month, he advised against it. I was put on limited activity. Other people should do the moving for me, and I should just sit on the couch and watch. We decided to make the move after my doctor helped us find another doctor who would take me on as a patient in Oregon.

We were moving to Oregon. I wasn't as sad to be moving from California to Oregon as I had been moving from Michigan to California. I think part of it was I didn't have family in California, hadn't developed close friendships yet, and didn't have a strong community at a church or elsewhere yet. I was moving from a place to which I didn't have strong ties yet. After only two years, I didn't feel as though I was leaving something, so moving just seemed like another adventure to me.

Matt went to Oregon a couple more times to get settled before I came out, since I wouldn't be able to do much. At six-plus months pregnant, I was on leave from work and on bed rest. I could only do little things to get ready for the babies' arrival. I did everything I could to keep them from coming any earlier than necessary. So I sat on the couch, read a lot, and waited.

On my first visit to Oregon, we had found a house and put a hold on it. On one of Matt's trips to Oregon, he decided to look around the area further because he wasn't sure he wanted to live in another neighborhood house. He wanted more. He found some property with an older house and a barn on just over twenty-one acres. He was so excited about it and the possibilities of raising a family there, and who knew what other stuff he could do?

What? I couldn't believe he had already decided to buy another place I hadn't even seen. *What does it look like? Can we move in when we get there?*

He raved about it and how much I would love it. "It's a great move, and we should do it." My life was moving too fast. I couldn't think about all these things; I needed to focus all of my attention on making sure I did everything I could to have a healthy pregnancy.

We packed up and moved to an apartment in Oregon that Matt's company put us up in. We now had only three months to finalize on a place to live, and I wasn't sure what Matt was doing. He took me for a ride to look at the farm and farmhouse. The property and house were a little rough looking and needed some work before we could move in. There was a small pond, a small peach orchard, a forest, and open fields for farming. The farm seemed a little far away from of lot of things, like the hospital, grocery stores, other neighborhoods—and everything else. I was all set to move into a new house and neighborhood, and now I had to switch my thoughts on everything. Where were we going to live?

We met the older couple that was selling the property, and then Matt took me for a ride on a rough, bumpy dirt road that went around the perimeter of the property. All I remember was how rough the ride was and telling Matt, "You need to get me off of this road right away, or we're going to have our twin boys right here and now." I was getting nervous about being bounced around so much, especially since I was trying to do everything I could to keep these babies in as long as possible before their due date. I told Matt right then and there he could do whatever he thought was best; I couldn't make that kind of decision in the state I was in.

I look back at it now, at what I told him, and see it as the beginning of him taking full advantage of doing whatever he wanted whenever he could. He would often have things all figured out, with his mind already made up, before letting me know what was up and then rushing me to make a decision right then.

He took me back to the house, and within a week we had bought a twenty-one-acre farm with an old farmhouse and a barn. I had no idea how we were going to get everything ready in time to move in before the twins were born. We decided to rent a house while we did some remodeling to the farmhouse. I eventually became excited about this new adventure, but at the same time, I didn't like feeling in transition and not being able to get our house and the boys' room ready before they were born.

I was in a new community and a new state again. Not being in a neighborhood, I was afraid I'd be alone a lot. I was going to be a new mom in a community where I didn't know anyone, on property that wasn't close to anyone or anything. I was excited to be a stay-at-home mom to my twin boys, but living on a farm away from people, I found myself feeling alone with the kids a lot. Matt had his work, farm projects he loved working on, and his family.

As the years went on, our family grew. It was hard for me to get pregnant the second time, and we turned to fertility drugs again. I became pregnant with our daughter, Molly. After she was born, I decided that was enough of taking fertility medication. I felt we were pushing it to have more kids, not only for my health but for what was best for our family as well. I was already so blessed to have three healthy, wonderful kids, even though I would have loved to have more.

Then, three years later, I was surprised to find out I was pregnant again with our fourth child, Jacob. I couldn't have been more thrilled and excited, not only because we were going to have another child but also because the pregnancy happened naturally, without help from any fertility drugs. Each time I was pregnant, we had the same chance of having an average-size baby or a dwarf baby. Zachary ended up being our only dwarf child; Jeremy, Molly, and Jacob were average-size children.

I thought life couldn't be any better. I was married to a man who always kept life busy and took care of his family, I was a mom to four great kids, and we lived on a farm that was the perfect place to raise a growing family. Everything seemed so perfect that I had to pinch myself to be sure this was my life. It wasn't exactly the life Matt and I had planned for, but we were fortunate to have it. We settled into our roles in our relationship as husband and wife, and as parents.

Of course being a mom changed my life, and I loved every phase of it—from being pregnant and then trying to bounce back to my normal self to the late-night feedings, the toddler stages, teething, teenager years, and all the in-betweens. I knew God had prepared me to be a mom. I have never felt more certain of anything in my life. The things I put myself through in my younger years and the challenges I faced all came down to preparing me for motherhood. God has always truly blessed me.

When I look back and think about some of the things I worried about when I was a teenager, I'm kind of sad. I'm sad about how much time I wasted over things that didn't really matter and the friends I kept at a distance because I was afraid to be vulnerable and allow anyone in. I thought too much about being different, that so many others seemed to have it better or easier than I did, and that I'd never quite look or be good enough. I feel like I missed out a little on those years, but over time, those years also helped me grow up and appreciate myself, other people, and life more.

As I faced each day, I overcame those challenges because somewhere within me I hung on to my faith and still believed in myself. I was able to have the right attitude and determination to tell myself I could do it. I learned how to push past some of those negative thoughts and just do what I needed to do.

A Little Me

It's much easier to give up than to try again and again, but try again we must. Giving up can't be an option, only changing directions. The challenges I've faced helped me understand that failure is a part of life, but so is success, and I have the ability to pick myself up and try again and again until I succeed. I remember my father telling me that my life is meant to be lived, to give and to serve. Everyone can do that. I almost chose the other way, to just give up and not live life anymore, but I didn't. I couldn't do that. I'm glad I had the strength to overcome the self-doubts and the challenges I had because I saw myself as a little person, not simply as a person like anyone else.

My life brought me here: married, a wife, a mom to four wonderful children, and a stronger woman. I grew up a lot and got outside of my comfort zone to appreciate a lot more in life. Marriage and being a mom had such a big and positive impact on my life, as well as having an impact on those around me. My kids showed me it wasn't just about me anymore; they helped me be aware of others and their needs and wants too. I found my purpose. I didn't always get things right, but my heart and intentions were always to be and give my best to my kids and family.

Marriage, moving to Oregon, living on our farm, and raising my kids truly were blessings in my life. Like my marriage did, being a mom to my four children changed my life forever. I'm a better person because of it in ways I could never fully explain. There is nothing else that has touched my heart in such an overwhelming way. I didn't have time or need to focus so much on what people thought, the what-ifs, or whether I was good enough or pretty enough. I had four blessings who were dependent on me, and I had to be the best mom I could be for them and a good wife/partner to Matt. I gained more confidence and strength than I ever knew I had before, and it helped me to face the challenges that lay ahead.

Like most marriages, we had our ups and downs, but we always seemed to come through those challenges better and stronger. Only the days ahead would tell.

Encouragement from Amy:

~Have a heart of joyfulness, gratitude, compassion, and love toward yourself and others. You'll be more fulfilled than if you look on the other side of the white picket fence, wanting what someone else has.

CHAPTER 13

Life's Ups and
Unexpected Downs

A Little Me

I've had a wonderful life since moving from Michigan to California, getting married, and then moving to Oregon and having kids. My life hasn't been the same since.

I was very happy and couldn't have imagined the life I was living with Matt on the farm. We had so many adventures—from everyday life to doing a reality show about our family. My life was going great, and I hoped it would be like it was for the rest of my life.

When Matt asked me to marry him and I said yes, of course we weren't sure what married life would be like. Who does? As a couple, you grow along with each other in each season of life, staying with it through thick and thin. That's a commitment, made in love, to your relationship. I wanted to take that adventurous journey with him, and I'm so glad I did. I loved Matt and being married to him, I loved being a mom, I loved living on our farm and being able to stay home to raise our kids—I loved my life. It wasn't perfect; in fact, we definitely had a roller coaster of a ride, but it was good.

Matt . . . I found someone I loved who helped me be a better me. He helped me take risks and be adventurous, and learn that everything doesn't always have to be known before you take a step. It's okay to be unsure. I thought we complemented each other. However, as I look back to the day I said yes and all that has gone on in my life since then, I couldn't have imagined I'd one day be a single woman again.

The one thing that didn't seem to change in all those years was the farm. It's crazy, I know—it's only a piece of land, real estate—but the farm we still own always seemed to be that seventh person in the family, and it had such a personal impact on my life and on our family. Though it was just a piece of land, that piece of land became a home and a part of us.

Amy Roloff

The farm changed over the years as we added lots more trees, landscaping, fixed up the barn and added two pole barns, and built all the extras, like a cowboy town. Even after twenty-eight years and all the changes to it and in my family, the farm feels the same as when we first moved here and has weathered tremendously well. It's a special place you get drawn to and don't want to leave. Yet, deep down, I know there will come a day when I may have to say goodbye. It saddens me to even think about the possibility of not living here one day. It's the only home I've known since we moved to Oregon. So many memories have been made here. This farm, where I raised my kids, was a big part of what made me who I am today. The thought of leaving someday reminds me of when I had to say goodbye to my childhood home in Michigan. This is where my married life and my children's childhood took place, and it's a place I hope my grandkids will experience one day. So for right now, this is where I plan to stay.

My twin boys, Jeremy and Zachary, were about four months old when we moved into the farmhouse after doing some basic remodeling. The day we moved in was an exciting day. I had looked forward to finally beginning to settle in and make it our home, as well as cooking in the new kitchen. The kitchen will always be my favorite place in my house because it's what I love to do, and it's one of my ways of expressing my love language.

After managing this first remodel to the house, Matt settled into his new job and, in his spare time, worked on projects around the farm. The farm was his baby. He loved driving the tractor, digging in the dirt, and building—just like a kid. He enjoyed his work and some of the traveling he had to do for it, but the farm fed his big creativity. He loved coming up with new remodeling projects for the house, building, tending to our small peach orchard, then planting our pumpkin patch, and managing the few farmhands we hired to help us make it all happen. Every time I turned around there was something new being built or done to the house or farm. I had my hands full with the kids, so I didn't pay too much attention to what he was doing on the farm, just as he probably didn't know all the everyday goings-on with the kids and me. It was a toss-up sometimes between his time at work as a software programmer in the tech industry, going out after work with colleagues and friends, and the farm—let alone family time. All of it kept him busy.

I enjoyed all that kept me busy—being home raising and spending time with our kids, becoming involved in school activities, church, and projects around the house. I'm so thankful I had the choice to be a stay-at-home mom. I wouldn't trade it for anything. My kids became my life, and the few friends I had were like family since I didn't have family nearby, which was hard for me personally. I felt a little lonely and isolated in those early years in Oregon. I chose to put myself aside and put my time into my kids, and it helped me to not dwell on not having family close by. I often missed interacting with people and having friends over, but like anything, it's hard to make connections with other people and develop friendships at first, but it gets easier over time.

Despite the isolation, I loved the quiet living out in the country; it was wonderful. I loved the property we had, and now I was glad I had told Matt, as he drove me around the farm when I was pregnant, "Do whatever you think is best." We both found our own routines. Excitement was always just around the corner, being married and sharing a life with Matt on the farm.

When the weather was bad the electricity would often go out. It was kind of exciting and fun when that happened, but we also knew we would be one of the last to get our electricity back on because the city and suburbs would be first. However, my kids loved when that happened. We'd light some candles, get out the flashlights, start a fire in the fireplace, have peanut-butter-and-jam sandwiches, and "camp out" in the house. My kids had a blast, especially when the chances of them not having to go to school the next day were high.

On a cold winter day, when the boys were nine months old, we got the biggest scare of our lives. My in-laws were visiting, and we were all hanging out in the family room talking, playing games, and watching an old movie. The farmhouse is a two-story house with the master bedroom on the main floor and the other bedrooms upstairs. I converted the dining room into the boys' temporary bedroom when they were babies, because I wanted them close so I could check in on them quickly. Since the boys were born prematurely at thirty-four weeks, I was afraid I might not hear them if their bedroom were upstairs. They would eventually move upstairs when they got a little older.

So on this particular night I stepped in to check on them, like I did every night, and all seemed well. About an hour later, my mother-in-law went to check on them and noticed Zachary didn't look right. Something seemed seriously wrong, and panic suddenly ensued.

She yelled for my father-in-law and Matt to come immediately. Zachary wasn't breathing and was turning blue, so she started CPR right away. Everything happened so fast. I think I was in shock, because I couldn't move. I was so scared. I started scrambling around trying to figure out what to do. Matt told me to call 9-1-1. Then he changed his mind and told his mom and me to get Zachary in the car because we were heading to the hospital. He didn't want to wait for the ambulance—that would take too long. Matt called 9-1-1 as we were getting in the car, but the dispatcher insisted we wait for the ambulance. They were on their way and would be there in seconds. Matt thought we could get to the hospital quicker ourselves than if we waited for the ambulance, but we ended up waiting, which seemed like a lifetime. The paramedics finally arrived and took over attending to Zach. Then he was rushed to the hospital.

It was agony waiting to hear what was wrong or happening to him. Would he be okay? Would he suffer any complications from not being able to breathe for those few moments? I was scared for him. I sat and prayed silently to the Lord that he would help Zachary get well and be just as feisty and strong as he was before this happened.

After the doctors performed a few tests and examined him, they finally came out and told us he would be okay but would need to stay in the hospital for at least a week. Zachary's life was saved by the EMTs' quick response. It didn't look like he would have any side effects from the whole ordeal. I have never been so relieved. I cried.

That was a hard night to go through, thinking our nine-month-old baby could have died or something could have been seriously wrong with his health. From that day on, I didn't sleep very well because I would check in on the boys often throughout the night to see if they were okay. The memory of that night still scares me when I think about it. We could have lost him. I'm thankful we didn't and that his health has been good ever since.

We found out Zachary had a bad virus, RSV (today there is a vaccination available for it), that got into his lungs and caused him to stop breathing. He couldn't get enough oxygen. I prayed he would not have any complications or brain damage from the lack of oxygen.

He was in the hospital for two weeks for monitoring and was put on nebulizer treatments for a while after that. I was so glad I had decided to make the dining room their bedroom. If we hadn't been able to react that quickly, he might not be with us today. I was so happy and thankful when we were finally able to bring him home. And it was comforting to know the farm wasn't as far away from everything we would need as we might have thought, after all.

As the years went by, our family got bigger, as did our house and farm. My daughter was born three years after I had Jeremy and Zachary, and my youngest, Jacob, was born three years after Molly. Another farmer helped us farm some of our land while we planted pumpkins for our new pumpkin patch in another area.

As if he didn't already have too much going on, Matt felt compelled to stretch his creativity by building fun things around the farm for the kids, like a western town, a tree house, a tunnel underneath the remodeled barn, and a castle.

My marriage, children, and family were the main focus in my life. I didn't have enough time to pursue other projects until my kids were older and involved in school and other activities. When they started school, I was the classroom mom and got involved in projects at their school.

When Jacob wanted to start playing soccer, like his siblings, I made the courageous decision to coach his team. I had never played soccer, and here I decided to coach. But after years of taking Jacob's brothers and sister to their practices and going to their games, I figured I knew a little something about the basics of the game, enough to coach a kindergarten team.

A Little Me

As the kids got older and more independent, the extra time gave me the chance to develop some relationships with other women, some of the moms of my kids' friends and others I met at school and church. I was known as the mom with the van who drove my kids, and everyone else's kids, everywhere. Many thought that, although our farm was wonderful and fun to hang out at, it was just too far away to visit. Similar to when I decided I wouldn't make distance an obstacle between Matt and me in our long-distance relationship, I didn't want distance to keep my kids' friends from coming over to play, so I drove back and forth a lot to make it happen. I was the chauffeur.

I continued to stay involved in my kids' lives as my twin boys got older and my two youngest began school: after-school activities, taking them to their sport practices, going to their games, homework at night, reading bedtime stories, and everything else that happens in family life. Matt and I continued in our marriage and parenting roles. He went to work and took care of the farm business, and I took care of the kids, the house, and family life. I did my best to bridge and balance these two parts of life, business and personal. But between work, farm projects, and family life, we didn't make enough time for us.

The kids loved playing and having adventures on the farm after school and on weekends. They loved riding on the Mule ATV with their dad and going berry picking with Mom. They had freedom to go off and find their own adventures in the forest, along the creek and railroad tracks, and with some of the things Matt built too. They loved playing in the dirt, riding ATVs, camping and hanging out by the fire, and using tools to build their projects. They loved to play soccer in the big grass field. They loved hearing the adventure stories their dad would make up or having me read their favorite books to them. Often the kids would go berry picking or pick peaches and bring them to me so I could make jam or a pie. I would know they'd already had a lunch of picked berries or peaches by the juice all over their shirts and hands.

I loved that my kids were learning how to play and had a place to do it big. They didn't have time to be bored. Jeremy and Zachary would get scraps of wood, branches, nails, and a hammer and build things. Jacob always hung around watching them, hoping for a chance to help. My boys would play with their G.I. Joes on the big rocks, the creek that ran through our farm, or in the forest, and come up with all sorts of scenarios of play. Molly loved to go wherever the boys went and would tag along with her American Girl doll or a G.I. Joe of her own. She also loved the sandbox, her bike, reading, and most all the things the boys did.

The kids—all of us, really—had a blast during the summertime, running through the sprinklers or sliding down the big hill on a long piece of plastic that we rolled out and ran the sprinkler on. My kids ran barefoot in the grass, and were fancy-free. The first several years, the kids loved swimming and splashing around in our pond. We had a paddleboat and a couple of inner tubes, and they would float around the pond pretending one of them was a pirate on a ship, chasing the others because they had stolen his or her loot. The imagination they had! Those were the Tom Sawyer and Huckleberry Finn kind of summers. They lived to play.

Farm life was idyllic for many years. It was one of the happiest of times. I loved where we lived and the opportunity to share our farm with others, whether for fundraisers, at our pumpkin patch, or just simply getting together. The farm was a part of the family, and in many ways it still is. There is something about the farm, like glue, that held our marriage and family together for many years and gave us many life lessons, experiences, and memories. Family is everything regardless of what is going on. It has been the perfect place to raise our four children and a place that has made a difference in others' lives as well. I was happy and felt very blessed to live such a life. We gave our kids a childhood like no other, one filled with wonderful adventures and unforgettable memories.

Life did move fast in those days, and I wonder what happened to that early family life on the farm that changed my marriage and my life so much. There were red flags that popped up in my relationship, which I either ignored or didn't want to see at the time. Perhaps a big factor was that Matt and I got too comfortable with our individual roles and forgot we needed to make time for each other.

After a number of years on the farm, we started another remodel on the farmhouse. It went through about a half-dozen different remodels before we said, "That's enough. We are done and we are good." During one of those remodels, I couldn't use the kitchen and the rooms were torn apart upstairs, so we all slept in one room for weeks. A remodel can be stressful on a marriage and family; everything seems out of sync, not to mention the extra financial cost. We made it through, though.

We kept up the small peach orchard on the farm for a number of years. I did the old mom-and-pop "u-pick" while Matt worked or traveled for work. The kids were still young then and would run around the farm and between the trees while I tended to the customers who came to pick peaches. It was wonderful to interact with and meet so many people.

Matt's time continued to be spent managing the farm, building really cool structures, and restoring the old barn. In his spare time, he and a few of our farmhands would tear down old barns so he could reclaim the rustic barnwood. We had a busy life—it's all I knew with Matt—but in a lot of ways, I think the busyness of life, in the long run, was a big distraction in our marriage and family life. Being too busy can make us miss a lot of the little things, which are important too.

Finding farmhands to help us on the farm didn't seem to be easy for Matt. One day he suddenly told me he had hired a man from Florida to help us out. And by the way, he would be living with us for a while, down in our basement.

What? Living where? You hired a guy to work on the farm, someone we don't even know, and he'll be living in our house? I couldn't believe it. I didn't remember having this conversation before. What was he thinking? What would I do if Matt had to travel for work and there was a man I didn't know living in our basement?

I found myself feeling that I needed to make it work even though I didn't have a say in any part of this crazy decision. It may not have been a bad decision, but I hadn't been included when it should have been both of us making it. Matt had already told the guy he could live with us and to come on out. It took me quite a while to feel even slightly comfortable about this decision. I eventually let it go and brushed it under the rug, as the saying goes. I didn't want to argue with Matt over decisions and choices he had already made. This became another red flag, one of many I had to watch out for. I felt I was beginning to not know what was happening on the farm and in the farmhouse I lived in.

A Little Me

In hindsight, I know I should have spoken up and talked about things that may have been tough for us, and expressed my feelings more often so Matt would've known how I felt, instead of just shrugging it off. I'm sure to Matt everything was good since I didn't speak up.

It took a lot for me to keep up with him and his many hurry-up, last-minute decisions. I liked hearing his ideas, many of which were good, but I also wanted a plan for how we were going to make it all work out, instead of just automatically going along with an idea and waiting to see what happened. I wasn't always expecting an absolutely no-problems-guaranteed plan but at least a plan with a general direction. These ideas and rushed decisions also required financial resources. Some of them made me feel disconnected from the farm and from my own life because I didn't feel like we were doing things together as much as we needed to. Maybe if I had, we could have discussed more things together and been on the same page before decisions were made without the other's input. Who makes the decision to have a stranger stay in your home without talking about it with the other person first?

The guy from Florida stayed with us for about three months, and then, *poof*, he was gone. It was a strange summer, and I was grateful everything ended up okay. It definitely made for another memorable summer on the farm.

Matt and I had the opportunity one year to take a combined trip to Las Vegas and Europe. He needed to attend events for his work in both places, and we turned the trip into a personal vacation as well. All the bright lights, architecture, and magnificent water features in Vegas were spectacular. While in Europe, besides the history, museums, spectacular architecture, castles, and food, we also found ourselves visiting Euro Disney. The ideas Matt drew from that trip were unique, to say the least.

Afterward, Matt decided to build a custom pool that would be unique, like something in Vegas or Disneyland, have a water slide and waterfall, and would be great fun for the family. Of course it sounded awesome and would have been nice, but I had a hard time convincing myself we needed a big, elaborate, and costly custom-built underground pool. Matt and his ideas were sometimes like trying to contain a toddler who wants everything in a candy or toy store. When he had an idea he was in his element and nothing could persuade him from not pursuing it.

To build this type of pool, he needed someone familiar with this type of design and construction. He found a guy who built elaborate pools in Las Vegas, and asked if he would consider coming to Oregon to build us one. After several discussions, not only did the builder say yes, he actually decided to move his whole family to Portland while he worked on our project. We thought this was a little odd for a "short-term project." Portland is not known for its sunny weather, let alone custom-built elaborate underground pools. Usually it drizzles or rains, and is wet, damp, and cold six or more months out of the year—at least, that's what we Oregonians tell people. I think it was all the hyped-up stories Matt told him about how beautiful and great Oregon and the Portland area were, how the summers were like California weather, that suddenly made him want to pick up and move his family from Vegas to Portland.

Another project I really didn't know much about, but Matt had made the decision and put it in motion.

A Little Me

The pool builder and his family came in late spring, and since they had nowhere to live yet, Matt said they could live in our barn while they looked for a place. The barn had water and a small bathroom, but that was about it. It was pretty rustic for a family to stay in longer than a day or two, but they stayed much longer than even Matt anticipated. They lived in our barn throughout the summer while the guy "built" our pool.

It took him forever to get anything started. There always seemed to be a reason why he got distracted or wasn't farther along on the project, such as not having the right supplies or not being able to find workers to help him. There were excuses after more excuses for why no real work had been made on it.

In the middle of this project, with this family living in our barn, we left for a couple of weeks on an already-planned family vacation. While on our way back home, we got a call from the builder letting us know his wife had just had a baby . . . in the barn . . . on our farm.

What? You're kidding, right? You just had a baby on the farm?

We were shocked, but excited for them at the same time. We asked if they had gone to the hospital, but he said no, he had delivered the baby and everything went well. We still insisted they go to the hospital right away to get checked out and make sure everything was okay, but they didn't want to. That seemed a little strange to me.

Afterward, I asked Matt, "What do you really know about this guy and his family?" He didn't know much about them, except he had seen some of the fancy pools he had built in Las Vegas. When we asked how the pool was coming along, he was a little vague on the details. We were anxious to get home to see their new baby girl, who was born on Roloff Farms, and see the progress he'd made on the pool.

When we arrived, we couldn't find them anywhere. We suddenly realized they were gone. *Poof!* We couldn't believe it. No word from them except the phone call we got on our way home to let us know about the baby. So on a warm, sunny summer day, the guy who was supposed to build us a custom pool left us with a big hole in the ground and a lump of concrete. We had no idea where they went. It was as if something beyond just having a baby caused them to up and leave without a word. We noticed, as we looked around the barn, that they must have left in a hurry because they left a number of personal items behind, but there was no sign they would be coming back. We wondered about the baby.

We had spent the whole summer looking forward to a custom pool, but there was only a half attempt made toward something that looked like a pool. If not for the big bowl-shaped glob of cement left behind in the ground, it sounds like some story we made up about an imaginary family that stayed in our barn and had a baby there. It was a very strange summer. We never heard from them again. We had spent some money to get this project off the ground, and we were left without a finished pool, but it made for a memorable story.

Over the years, we opened up our farm to a lot of people and to the community for various events, class parties, company picnics, and nonprofit fundraiser events besides having our own personal time, like the kids' birthday parties and having friends over. Matt got the farm ready with our farm help, and I enjoyed being the host. We made the farm our home, but enjoyed sharing it with many others as well. The farm gave us another purpose in life. Our little pumpkin crop was the beginning of a bigger, more successful pumpkin patch later. The peach orchard and the pumpkin patch brought many families and individuals to the farm.

Matt suddenly decided one day—at least, it seemed that way—to tear out the entire peach orchard in order to expand the pumpkin patch. I couldn't believe he didn't prepare me for that. The kids and I loved the peach orchard, and we were upset over losing it. We would never taste a more delicious peach than the ones we picked from our trees.

Matt often did impulsive things without letting me know ahead of time. He would say he had a plan, not to worry. I wished he had at least kept a few trees for the family. Often his impulsiveness was hard on me because it came unexpectedly, making me more reactionary than reasonable. I didn't have time to think about or feel like a part of projects that would have an impact on me and the kids, and the family as a whole. And I didn't like the feeling I got.

The pumpkin patch has grown ever since and, in the end, became a thriving business for us. I enjoyed playing host to all the families that came out to have a fun farm experience. Matt, along with managing a number of workers, did a lot of work to get the farm ready and maintain it for opening day of pumpkin season at Roloff Farms. But it was worth it.

I thought we made a good team, even if we did get off to a rough start. Matt was in his element, making all the logistics come together to complete a project like this, and I loved being in my element, greeting and helping individuals and families. The kids even liked the patch and helped out when they could. The farm continued to be like an extended family member, and we enjoyed sharing it with others. People came from all over to visit the farm. When Matt and I complemented each other, we did it well. He had the creative talent to build it and pull it off, and I added a dose of reality and the hospitality to make everyone feel welcome.

The farm—a place where my kids got to play, build forts, ride around on ATVs, have friends over, walk barefoot in the grass, have campfires, build, learn to drive a lawn mower and tractor, and so much more. It was also a place other people loved to visit. When the kids were growing up was a happy, memorable, and adventurous time. The farm was family, and the family was the farm.

I love the farm I live on, and its open space. I like the smell of hay, hearing the frogs in the evening, hearing the train go by early in the morning or late at night, seeing the beautiful sunsets, and actually being able to see so many stars at night. I loved being married to Matt, and I loved being a mom. All three events in my life were significant because each gave me a different kind of growth in confidence and strength. Maybe it was because I had others to love, think about, and put my time and focus into instead of my insecurities, uncertainty, and thoughts of *I'm not good enough*. I redirected my focus from being inward, on myself, to being outward, and did my best to put more into other people, like my kids, family, and friends.

Unfortunately, time will also change things, people, and our environment when we least expect it. I found myself looking back and wondering what happened in my life and marriage. I didn't handle certain situations as well as I wanted. Looking back, I see red flags I missed. Perhaps I didn't want to see them because then I wouldn't have to deal with them. I see how I changed and yet became more critical of myself. I let what-ifs creep back into my life, which affected how I saw myself and how I looked at life. My environment, my home life and marriage, began to change in a way I was not prepared for. Although we had many good times, it wasn't easy to overcome the challenges in our marriage. It had its hills and valleys, and for a while we made it work.

Over time, many discussions I had with Matt eventually made me feel less than. He may not have meant or realized how his words, businesslike attitude, and lack of compassion affected our relationship and me. But they did. To him, my projects and interests didn't seem big enough or good enough, or weren't worth the time to pursue them. And so the what-ifs crept back into my mind in a way that made me feel less than. I was mad at myself for allowing that to happen; it seemed I let it happen often, and I didn't know why. It affected not only myself but everything I held dear. His words stayed in my mind and played with my emotions, and I sometimes became intimidated by Matt with his strong and domineering personality. I just didn't get the support and encouragement I needed to be able to communicate with him in such a way that he actually heard, cared about, and listened to what I said.

Something was missing between us, and I was figuring out my part in it. Matt moved quickly and figured things out later. Whatever it was, he plowed ahead. If I wasn't ready or needed more information before making a decision, he couldn't wait for me and would roll right on past. We became worse at communicating with each other and had different views on our finances. The top two challenges that can cause stress, tension, and hardship in any marriage—communication and finances—we had them.

Matt's tremendous creativity was infectious, but it was also demanding and did lend itself to impulsiveness. I was intimidated by it. I let a lot of things get brushed under the rug instead of dealing with them. I can still hear him say, "We must do this," or "We really need to buy this," or "We can't let this opportunity slip by." I remember him saying he was going to die early; he needed to do things now. I needed to think about all the options so that I could feel good about making those kinds of decisions, not make them in haste. And I admit I took some time, longer than necessary sometimes, to make a decision. I don't know anyone who has an unlimited treasure chest they can dig into, and his projects took a lot of money.

Meanwhile, my dreams got swept under the rug. I was slipping away a little bit at a time. I felt a part of my kids' lives and Matt's life, family life, but I didn't have just a little bit of a life of my own. Each time I thought about this, I felt a little selfish. Matt and I were facing a number of things in our relationship, but three specific issues we faced, which can make any marriage difficult, were finances, communication, and allowing life to get in the way. My marriage was up and down, wonderful and difficult, all at the same time, but I truly hoped everything would work out for the best in time.

I think Matt and I got a little too comfortable in our separate roles. Matt was the breadwinner and managed the farm, while I was the stay-at-home mom who took care of the kids, house, and family. Our marriage wasn't the biggest priority anymore, and we got lost.

My relationship reminded me of a sailboat: You plan for a trip and make sure you have all the tools and resources, like a compass, to navigate and sail in calm or rough waters. You prepare to handle any situation that arises. If not, when storms suddenly come up, it's not the time to realize you're going in the wrong direction or that you don't have what you need or know how to use the tools that would help you weather the storm and get where you need to go. And you wonder, *Is it too late to find my way back?* No, it should never be too late to find your way back.

We both needed to make a plan together. Our priorities got all mixed up. Life had become more about business, and I thought we needed more personal time with each other. We were losing our compass, the compass we needed to navigate our marriage and life. We lost faith. I hoped we would find our way back to a stronger us together. It was my marriage on the line, and it was worth trying to figure out how. You don't run away when the going gets tough. I tried to hang on as best I could and have the faith that we would make it together.

My positive takeaway is that a marriage always needs to be put first. The rest will follow and be stronger because of it. We both lost that over time in our own ways. The question was, could I get it back?

Encouragement from Amy:

~We need to do the personal part of life as well as the business part. Both are important and necessary. However, don't let the business of life become so important that it squelches the personal and takes away the little joys in life. It's about balance, and when one dominates most of the time, the other will suffer.

CHAPTER 14

Real Reality

A Little Me

When social media became such a prominent element in all our lives a number of years ago, it reminded me of our show, *Little People, BIG World*. All of it is real life, but what is the reality we want to show others? The same applies to what we decide to post on social media—what is real and what is perceived as real?

I wasn't quite aware, in the beginning, of the impact our show had on others or on myself, and how social media would influence what we were doing. By the time I figured it out, social media was everywhere.

My youngest son posted some pictures on Instagram showing his perspective of filming and his family. When I saw them, I could better understand his perspective and the impact filming had on his young life. For the majority of his life, and much of his brothers' and sister's lives, we had been filming our show about our family. He may not have expressed it clearly, but I understood what he was trying to say. When I was asked about his post while being interviewed on a local TV show, I became mama bear and told them yes, he was correct. He saw an edited version of his family and not enough of real "normal." We were real and what we filmed was real, but the editing of our show influenced what people saw. The story was real, but editing can change the story—at least from my perspective.

What we choose to post on social media reminds me somewhat of the editing process of TV. We usually take a selfie when we are at our very best, to show ourselves in the very best light. After we take the picture and post it, we generally go back to what we were doing, just normal-life stuff. Sometimes normal is boring, and we think, *Who wants to see normal?* Are both times real—the carefully selected, edited selfie and normal life? Yes, of course they both are. Yet we often don't want anyone to see the other side, what the edited selfie usually doesn't show—real life. That's how I would describe our show, Little *People, BIG World*. It's real, but by the time you see it, it's an edited version of real.

Sometimes *real* became a little too real. We had some great and memorable times filming, but some trying times as well.

This chapter is hard to write because it's about a time and a relationship in my life that started out wonderfully but ended up how I never imagined it would. The experience changed me. Half of my life was normal, and then I realized the other half felt kind of like a selfie. *What is real or not real, and why don't we talk about it? So how real should I get?* I will admit I wasn't good at filtering myself (so I was often told by Matt, and sometimes he was right). And sometimes things got taken the wrong way or completely out of context. It was difficult for me to determine what needed to be a filtered in what I said—*how can I still be real and still tell a real story?*

Throughout our first dozen years or so, we went through the typical things married couples go through. We made many happy memories, but we also differed in how we thought about finances, spending time with each other, outside friendships, raising our children, and the expectations we had for our relationship. We thought we were doing things pretty well. Then life seemed to change. What happened? Little challenges seemed to become bigger ones.

When Matt got laid off from work, it stretched us financially. It was a tough time for him, not working, and for me. I supported him as best I could while he looked for another job or a different line of work. He was always good at finding something.

After looking for a while without success, Matt decided to take a break from looking for a full-time job and do something totally different before moving on. He decided to run for the president's position of a nonprofit organization we both belonged to, Little People of America. He had thought about it and been in conversations about it for months. I commended him for wanting to take on such a big role and knew he would do a fantastic job, but was he serious about it? This was a scary and uncertain time for us, with him not having a steady job and income coming in, though he was on unemployment and did some consulting work to fill in the gap. We had debt to pay off and expenses to keep up with. This wasn't a paid position, and it would take up a lot of his time. I wondered what I could do to help out.

We started to talk about a big what-if: selling the farm if something didn't come up soon, because we wouldn't be able to keep up with the expenses. We had to consider how much longer we could live on and maintain the farm on our current income, or if we needed to do something totally radical, which neither of us really wanted to think about—sell the farm.

I know changes and unexpected things happen in life and in marriage, but it doesn't make it any easier going through them. The farm was our home, and it would be hard to move away. Our finances were becoming strained, and it was a tough time in our relationship. Talking about finances is not always an easy thing for couples, and it certainly wasn't for us. Yet, in the position we were in, we didn't really have a choice, though we should have communicated more about them and about our expectations for each other and our relationship. Were they realistic, or did they put additional pressure on us? But we let the opportunity to do that slip away. The president position was a two-year commitment that took up a lot of Matt's time. Where would working a full-time job fit in? It was tough, him not working, because Matt really did do a great job as president and accomplished a lot of good things for the LPA and its members.

When Matt set his mind on something, nothing else seemed to matter. Projects were like adrenaline to him, driving him hard. If something better came along, then he was on to the next new thing. Risk motivated him, and he thrived on being the underdog. He created challenges because "why not? Challenges build up resilience," which is very true. He felt people often underestimated him, and he was going to prove them wrong no matter what. It's one of the things I liked about Matt. He wasn't afraid of much of anything. However, with that focus, he forgot about others around him sometimes. You were either on board, or if not, he'd find someone else to bring on board.

I will admit, I'm not a big risk-taker and I don't feel the need to create additional challenges—life is full of them all by itself and will build up your resilience just by living it. I was motivated by accomplishing projects as well, but I also thought we needed more time with each other. My family, my kids, friends, cooking, doing projects around the house, school, raising monies, and church were my motivating elements. His drive and my desire to help others—I thought we complemented each other.

However, our relationship was slipping away. Little by little, we seemed to head in separate directions. We got lost in doing our own things. But I hoped and believed we would find our way back to each other. We needed to step back and take a look at where we were, where we wanted the relationship to go, and what we needed to do about it.

A Little Me

Everything came to a head after having a disagreement over money and where it was all going. Matt told me if I thought we didn't have enough money and it was so easy to find work, then why didn't I go out and find something to do besides just staying at home. I was hurt at his assumption that I wasn't doing anything at home or trying to keep things together for the family. He was harsh and intimidating.

I hadn't worked outside the home for years, but if that was what I needed to do, then I'd do my best to find a job. I really didn't know where to begin. It was going to be a challenge, but I told myself, *I can do this.* I hoped I would find something *I wanted* to do and not just a job. Whatever it was, I hoped it would help out enough to buy us a little more time to figure things out so that we didn't have to consider moving off the farm.

I put the word out to everyone I knew that I was looking for work. I took on Matt's challenge, and in the end, I'm grateful for it because it helped me realize I can do a lot more than I give myself credit for. Something that felt overwhelming ended up being something positive.

A good friend of mine was trying to fill a preschool teacher position for the upcoming school year and said I should apply for it. When Jacob was in kindergarten, I was his soccer coach and her son was on Jacob's team. She had seen how I coached and interacted with the players on the team and their parents, and thought I would be a perfect preschool teacher. So I applied and was very excited when I ended up getting the job several weeks later.

I had let a lot of what-ifs get in the way of my life, and I didn't want that to happen again. During my college years, I didn't go after a teaching degree because I let what-ifs get in the way. I threw those what-ifs out the window because I now had an opportunity to do something I had always wanted to do: teach and be with kids. I couldn't wait for the school year to begin.

I ended up getting not just one job but two. I had been involved in our local soccer club for a long time, with my other three kids playing the game and coaching Jacob's team, when another friend of mine, who was the fields manager for the club and my boys' coach at their school, asked if I would be interested in applying for the admin position they had open. I told him I was very interested, and I hoped I would get the position, but I wondered, *Will I have the time and be able to handle working two part-time jobs, coaching, and being a mom to my kids?* I'd think about that later—*let's see if I even get it.* I applied and did end up getting the position.

It had been a long time since I'd worked outside the home, and now I had two part-time jobs in a matter of weeks after Matt suggested I go out and look for work. I was so proud of myself for taking on a daunting challenge head-on. It made me realize again how important my attitude is in everything I do. I could've allowed this challenge to defeat me before I even started, or I could let it push me to know, *I've got this, so let's go out there and do it.* I went out with a purpose—to find work to help my family with our finances—and I was successful. I hoped I would still give enough time to my kids and family. Only time would tell. I would do my best to make it all work.

I loved teaching and being with kids. I regretted not pursuing a teaching degree in college, but teaching preschool gave me a second chance, and I wasn't going to let it slip by this time. I loved everything about teaching—from meeting the kids on the first day of school to teaching them all sorts of new things and seeing the joy on their faces when they accomplished something like reading, an art project, or making a new friend. I loved watching them interact with each other on the playground and in the classroom. You learn so much about your students then.

Some of the kids were a little scared, timid, and confused when they first met me. They would ask why their teacher was so short and why they were almost as tall as me. Why was I so different and funny looking? Was I a mama, and if so, why wasn't I tall like theirs? How could I be a teacher when I looked like a kid? Did I drive a car? Yep, I got all those inquisitive questions, and I loved each one because they were so innocent and curious. It was a great opportunity to share that it's okay to be different, because we all are. At first, some of the kids were afraid of me because I was a dwarf and looked very different, and I worried they wouldn't want to come to preschool anymore because of it. After several weeks went by, though, the kids began to get more comfortable with me and with the routine of school, and everything went fantastically the rest of the year.

Every year, with each new group of kids, I would get all the same questions again, and I would gladly tell each class I was different and short, but I was also a teacher and an adult even though I might not look like their moms. I was so happy to have them in my class and told them we were going to have a blast in school. I might be taller than them right then, but by the end of the year some of them would be taller than me, an adult. The kids liked being able to give me a hug and look at me face-to-face, and would often come up to me to see if they were getting taller. And by the end of the preschool year a few students would be as tall as me, which was the coolest thing to them. Years later, when I would see my former students, they would smile when they told me they remembered what I had said to them. I loved teaching and would have taught for the rest of my life if I could have. I miss it to this day.

Working for the soccer club was a good job as well. It gave me the opportunity to interact with parents, kids, coaches, and others in the community and gain office work experience. I got to know all the familiar faces I'd see on the field during games and practices. While working for the club and still coaching Jacob's team, I found out I loved coaching because it was similar to teaching.

Back when I first began coaching Jacob's team, when he was in kindergarten, a lot of those boys were just about my size as well, and I got the same questions from them as I did from the preschoolers now. I hoped by the end of the season they would think I was a pretty good soccer coach, for a little mom, even if they were taller than I was. I knew each year some of the parents would question if I could handle a team of boys, whether kindergarteners or twelve fourth-grade boys; just as the parents of my students wondered if I could handle a classroom of fifteen to eighteen preschoolers. Was I capable and did I know enough about the game to coach their sons? Parents want their kids to be on a winning team, even in kindergarten.

Again I had to prove, not only to myself but to the parents as well, that I'd be a good coach, win or lose. The players would always be my priority, though, not winning. Of course I wanted to win, just not at the cost of a player not having fun playing the game.

What was sometimes scarier and more intimidating was facing a bunch of dads, bringing their sons to practices and games, who thought they could coach the team along with me. I couldn't let that happen and diminish my authority with the kids. They probably knew a whole lot more about sports than I did, but I knew about kids too. When the opposite team saw a little woman coaching a boys' team, I'm sure the coaches/dads were thinking this was going to be a piece of cake. Well, they thought wrong. It just made me try even harder to be a good coach to those boys.

Coaching showed me again how people—even I, myself—will sometimes underestimate me. I wasn't going to allow myself to get caught up in the what-ifs or what others thought about me this time. Competing in DAAA sports all those years ago, I found out I'm competitive if I need to be. I can and will rise to the occasion, especially when others are counting on me like these boys were. I encouraged Jacob and the other players that playing a sport isn't just about winning, but about going out on the field and playing their best. I didn't want them to look back and have any regrets. It wasn't just about themselves; their team was counting on them as well. If they did their best, they couldn't ask anything more of themselves and they were already winners. I ended up coaching many of these boys through their fourth-grade year.

When Jacob tried out and made it on a competitive team, my recreational coaching days came to an end. I was so proud of him, and I was glad to be back on the sidelines rooting for him just as a mom. Everyone needs to know someone is cheering for them in whatever they do, and I hoped my kids always knew I was cheering for them.

Looking for work gave me the push I needed to find my confidence again, to know I could do more. I found my passion in both teaching and coaching, and loved being able to make a difference in kids' lives. What an opportunity I had to teach kids about the physical differences in people, to be kind and respectful toward others and themselves. I wanted them to see we are all similar on the inside, not focus so much on how we are different on the outside. It was a learning experience for me as well. My two jobs didn't cover all of our financial needs, but it gave us more time to figure out what we should do next.

***

We found ourselves in the news back in 1999, following a book Matt wrote about his life. I found it surprising that a lot of people seemed to be interested in my family. To me we were just like any other family. Perhaps we were unique since three of us were little people and three of us were average height.

People often ask why I use the term *average height* instead of *normal*, and *little people* instead of *dwarf*. *Little people* is a term generally accepted by most people with dwarfism. It doesn't really matter to me either way, *little person or dwarf*. I say *average height* instead of *normal* because I'm not "un-normal" because I'm a dwarf, I'm just different. We're all normal in our own way. The term *midget* is considered derogatory because of how the meaning has changed over the years into something that makes a person less than; it can come across as harsh and mean.

Then something I would never have imagined happened. In 2003 a TV producer reached out to Matt, wanting to know if we would be interested in doing a documentary-type reality show about our family. We would be one of three families featured in this show.

WHAT? A reality show? What does that mean?

Reality shows were pretty new back when we started, not like today with the slew of reality shows out there. A film crew would film the daily goings-on of a family that was kind of different and lived on a farm.

Matt was very interested in this idea. He came to me all excited about this "fantastic, once-in-a-lifetime" business opportunity and wanted to know if I would be on board.

He had an extremely persuasive personality and was very convincing that we should do it. He made everything he wanted to do sound fantastic, and most of the time it was.

I have to admit, my immediate response was a flat-out NO. No, I did not want to be a part of a reality show entitled *America's Strangest Families*. I didn't think there was anything strange about us. Again and again he tried to persuade me what a great thing this would be for the whole family. Again, I said no. I didn't want my family to be labeled as strange. I was also concerned about our ability to withstand the public scrutiny of our personal and family lives that would inevitably occur. I didn't feel as if I had the emotional strength to go through something like that, and I didn't think our relationship could withstand it either.

It was important to me that we had someplace where we could all just be ourselves and unwind. I wanted us to know, when we stepped out the front door, that we had a safe haven and a family that supported and loved each other to come home to. Once that door was flung open to filming, our personal life would be on view to the public, so then where could we go? I didn't think our home would be our home anymore, and how would we get that back? Our family had enough challenges in it just living regular life and raising kids. And now we would add a reality show to the mix? I worried about which one would take priority—our marriage and family, or a marriage and family on display for a reality show.

At the time this opportunity came to us, Matt was managing the farm and doing some consulting work but not working full-time, and I was still teaching, working for the soccer club, coaching Jacob's soccer team, and trying to be a good mom to our kids. How would we fit filming into our lives? Even though I didn't make a lot of money and was tired all the time, I really enjoyed what I was doing and didn't want to quit my two jobs. I wanted the kids to have a normal life, and I didn't think filming a reality show would provide that. Matt was convinced this was a once-in-a-lifetime opportunity financially and for the family, and something we couldn't pass up. He also thought we would be able to use this opportunity to advocate and make a difference in how others see people with dwarfism. He had a very good point on that note, and I was all about that. We may be physically different, but we're really just like everyone else.

If we took this on, I wanted him to understand why it would be hard for me to quit what I loved doing, but he couldn't see why it would be when we could be making a lot more money while doing more things on the farm. Besides, we could be a part of something that might make a difference not only for us but in other lives as well. Couldn't I do both, work and film? Why couldn't he see that? I still wasn't totally convinced. I worried that an image and brand would become more important than our personal life, and our personal life would then become all business. I already felt that we were too businesslike as it was. The what-ifs came up again because this decision affected more than just me and him; it would also affect our kids.

After repeatedly being asked by Matt to do the show, I finally gave in. Let's do it! Maybe he was right: maybe we could make a difference in how others perceived little people. BUT: I wanted to be sure that we could just be ourselves and keep our life and the kids' lives as normal as possible. I didn't expect the show to last more than a season or two, so I kept working the two jobs I had and coaching.

Here we were—a marriage, a family, a farm, and a reality show. What a combination! The door into our lives was thrown open for all to see the crazy, wonderful imperfections of a regular yet different family.

I was a little scared at the thought of filming. Could we really just be ourselves all the time? Or would we feel we could only be a version of ourselves when filming? And like taking a selfie, everyone didn't need to see all the dirty laundry about our life aired on TV. We had some really great experiences as a family, but it was hard not to show some of the rough times and the imperfections as well. I didn't want to start worrying about what the public thought of my family or of me and get caught up in being a people pleaser again. It was going to be a tough balancing act between real life and an edited version of reality for a TV show.

We filmed the pilot episode for *America's Strangest Families* in 2004. I still was not comfortable with that title; it bothered me a lot. I was thankful when the TV network turned down the pilot, and I thought we were done. Whew! But the producer came back to us wanting to do another pilot for a show with just our family. I still didn't want to do it, but maybe it would go better since it was just about our family. So we filmed another pilot in 2005, and months later found out a network had picked up the pilot and about six episodes that would air in 2006. Really? I couldn't believe it. We received the contract for our show entitled *Little People, BIG Dreams,* and I signed it. Later the title would change to *Little People, BIG World.*

After we signed, Matt called a family meeting to let us know his plans for making this work. He believed we shouldn't really talk to or trust any of the producers or crew because they didn't really care about us. We weren't their priority, making a TV show was, and they'd say anything to appease us to get what they wanted. It would be best if everyone in the family went through Matt about everything, and he would communicate with the production staff on our behalf and take care of everything.

From the start, I didn't think this was a good way to handle the situation. It would set a precedent of mistrust, creating an unfriendly home and working environment. *If we can't trust any of them, then why are we saying yes to filming and having them in our lives, in our home, and on our farm?* That just didn't make sense to me. We needed to be able to talk freely among ourselves and to the producers in order to have a collaborative atmosphere. I was still working two jobs at the time, getting only about four hours of sleep at night, and taking care of the kids, and sadly I didn't have as much time to figure out these kinds of details right then. So most everything related to the show did go through Matt.

In hindsight, I think I made a big mistake in not making myself more involved. It may have been good in the beginning for the business of the show, but not personally. We started filming our first season in 2006, and it aired later that year.

I could never have imagined having a reality show about our life and having people watch it. The blurring of real reality with an edited version of reality for a show made it hard to distinguish what was real or not in my life. It was like living two different yet similar lives in one. What happened off camera seemed a little different than what aired on camera, and yet in some crazy way, it was all still real life.

The challenges of family life for two little-people parents raising four children, one of them a little person and the other three average size, was just normal life to me.

Oddly enough, I think our relationship lasted longer because of the show than it probably would have otherwise, since we seemed to talk more on camera then we did off camera. We talked about storylines and what was going on in our lives. I don't remember us really talking about the episodes with each other, either beforehand or after we filmed them, to see if we were still on the same page about what was said and what we did. Matt knew a lot of what was going on—what the producers wanted in the episodes and what he was going to do. It often caught me off guard when the cameras were rolling.

It finally dawned on me that the edited version was different than what was filmed. All of it was real life, but when you film for two hours or more, they can't air the complete two hours that were filmed—everyone would be bored watching it, I'm sure. So when a scene was edited down to, say, a minute of footage, it came across much differently than how it felt in real time.

My takeaway from filming is we definitely should have talked more about what we filmed and critiqued it together. Matt seemed more concerned about what the fans were saying and what he read on the Internet than how we felt about it. Matt and I were still in the same book, but we just seemed to be in different chapters. So when people ask me if our show is "real," I say, "Yes, it is, but you're watching an edited version of real."

The show went from six episodes the first season to a second season with eight to twelve episodes to several seasons where we filmed

twenty episodes each. For several years, we were filming forty episodes, five days a week, ten months a year. Now, *that* is a job!

Filming *Little People, BIG World* became our main source of
income and the focus of our life on the farm. We forgot about the
cameras and always having people around after a while. We didn't
know anything different, really. The crew became friends we worked
with. It was hard for me to think "I couldn't trust them" and that
they "wouldn't do well by my family" because "it was just their job
and this was business." Matt would get upset if, after filming and off
camera, I'd be talking to the producers. I felt conflicted because he
did it all the time. I wasn't sure what the issue was about me doing
the same.

And I thought we would be finished in two seasons, yet here we
are in our fourteenth season at this writing and over three hundred
episodes later. I realize now what an impact our story and show had
not only in my life but in so many other lives as well. I finally got
what Matt had seen from the beginning. He saw an opportunity for
us to advocate and educate other people about dwarfism and differences by sharing our story about a family that looked different but
was just like theirs. We loved each other and had dreams, passions,
goals, successes, failures, adventures, and good and tough times. We
were an average, "normal" family.

After the first couple of years of filming, I finally had to tell myself, *I can't do all of this anymore.* I decided to quit my position at
the soccer club before another soccer season began in January 2008.
And in May I finished up the year teaching preschool. Since Jacob
had made it on a competitive soccer team beginning the following
fall, my coaching days ended in May as well. I had to let go of everything I came to enjoy and love doing to be there more for my kids

and my family, and so I could go on a different journey—filming real life with my family on our reality show.

So much happened those first several years. Our farm was thriving as our pumpkin patch grew bigger and bigger each year as more and more people visited during October. Matt took over the finances when I started working, and we soon realized we needed more farm help and office support to help us manage it all. So in late 2007 we hired someone to help us manage our pumpkin patch season. She did such a great job helping us with pumpkin season in 2008 that we hired her on as our farm manager soon afterward.

We had ups and downs in our marriage, like anyone else, but after several years of filming our show, I felt as if we were just going through the motions of a married couple most of the time. I'm more of a realist (or worrier), and Matt was more of a dreamer. Even though our personalities were different, I thought they would be more of a strength in our marriage than not. Yet we continued to slowly drift apart. Before the show began, we did try to keep our marriage together by finding resources on relationships and going to counseling, but nothing seemed to connect or work for us.

I went back to what I often do when I feel alone, lost, or overwhelmed: I slowly built a guarded wall around myself, like a fortress, really, to protect myself emotionally and hang on to what confidence I had in myself so I wouldn't get hurt. I stuffed my emotions deep down and pretended I could handle it and everything was okay. I know now that I let the little things go too often instead of communicating what bothered me. I swept things underneath the rug, per se.

Well, sometimes it's better to be hurt than to avoid a conversation or hide from what's going on. Sometimes a decision needs to be made instead of thinking, if you wait long enough, you won't have to decide and it will all just go away. Sometimes you need to say no and change directions for the sake of yourself and your relationship. Having tough conversations isn't easy, but they are necessary.

We ended up putting each other on the defense instead of in a collaborative "let's work this out together" position. We were losing the ability to communicate because we talked at each other instead of *to* each other. My marriage and family were the most important relationships in my life, and I didn't know how to get them back on track.

We became more frustrated and critical about everything between us. Being critical of myself wasn't healthy either. It was hard to face the personal things that were going on, as well as my part in them. Matt seemed to avoid our problems by going out every night and focusing his attention on his farm projects, other businesses, and other people. I kept my thoughts to myself. I tried hard to be what I thought he wanted in a wife, but in the process, I lost a little bit of myself. I was alone at home a lot, and my friends were there for me as best they could.

Unfortunately, the glue that kept us together wasn't really our relationship, but our children and the farm. We forgot that it takes faith, work, and sacrifice to have a good marriage. It's the one relationship that holds everything else together—not family, kids, friends, work, or projects, but each other in a marriage. We needed to want to work on it more than anything else that was going on in our life, but it got pushed farther down the list of priorities.

The reality show became a huge distraction for us. *Little People, BIG World* became a huge success, but our personal relationship was falling apart.

It's hard for me to watch our show because I don't always want to relive moments from six months or so ago, although I did like the scenes my kids were in and loved seeing them and hearing what they said in their interviews. Many unexpected life moments got filmed that I may not have always wanted to be shown publicly.

For instance, there was a harrowing pumpkin accident involving my youngest son and a good friend of ours who helped us with a few projects and eventually became Matt's business partner. It happened on the last day of pumpkin season. The pumpkin trebuchet malfunctioned, and suddenly Jacob and our friend were hurt. At that very second, we weren't sure how serious it was, the severity of their injuries, or if we had possibly just lost Jacob or our friend. Thankfully, their injuries weren't as severe as we feared. I was never so terrified or stunned, and everything around me seemed to be in motion except me. It was a terrifying moment for this mom. They were both rushed to the hospital in an ambulance, and Jacob did need surgery because he got hit in the head near his eye and chin. I prayed he would be okay. I was so scared about the possibility of him having brain damage or losing an eye. But thankfully the doctors were able to fix him up and he healed well.

Another sensitive area was filming about Zach's personal life being a dwarf. Zach didn't like the limelight, so talking about personal things wasn't easy for him.

Yet another difficult subject was Matt getting a DUI and having to go to court. It was hard on him and on me. It was difficult being in court and listening to the trial while having cameras on me, hearing the questions being asked and the answers given, sitting in the hallway with reporters and people all around me and hearing them talk about me, my husband, and our family as if I weren't there. I felt as if I were silently on trial as well. I had to be brave through it all and ignore it because I couldn't say anything.

When social media became prevalent, a lot of horrible, nasty things were said about me, my kids, and my family. It was incredibly hard to stay confident and not listen to or read what others said about us. I remember reading cruel things said about my daughter and her appearance when her brother Jeremy posted a picture of her in high school for a photography project. I just couldn't believe some of the things I read about my beautiful, precious daughter. I hoped she didn't read them and wouldn't be too hurt or affected by them. How could I be there for her?

Then the unimaginable happened: divorce. Going through a devastating personal event in the public eye was the toughest thing I ever had to go through as a wife, mom, and woman. Yet we had made our personal life public business, so why wouldn't this be a part of it? Sometimes I just wanted to hide behind closed doors and forget about it for a little bit.

There were also many wonderful opportunities and moments that came from filming. I will always be grateful for those times. Filming our life was like a seesaw: we were up one moment and then down the next. Highlights included the many trips we took as a family and the places we got to go, such as Hawaii, Australia, Costa Rica, Europe for the World Dwarf Games, the riverboat cruise on the Mississippi River, and Nashville. The best part was the wonderful people we got to meet along the way.

Of course, the income from the show allowed us to do many things. We did two major remodels to the farmhouse in 2006 and 2008, we were able to build up college accounts for our kids, and we got to do more things for the farm and our pumpkin patch. Thanks to filming, we were able to share our farm with many more people.

When we were asked to be a part of the Make-A-Wish Foundation, I was blown away. Out of all the people and places many of the kids and adults could have wished for, they picked our family and Roloff Farms to visit. What humbling and very inspiring moments those were to me.

We did what we did for several reasons, but to me the most important one will always be that we got to inspire at least one person, if not thousands. That is what kept me together and my feet on the ground to stay humble and thankful. The kids' birthday parties, Molly giving her eighth-grade valedictorian speech, the boys' last soccer game as seniors, being able to give back to kids when I started the Amy Roloff Charity Foundation, and just seeing my kids grow up to become the wonderful adults they are—these are some of the highlights I treasure.

We did make a difference through our show, and we continue to do so. I'll always be grateful that we got to share our story on TV. Because of it, I got to meet so many wonderful people around the country and in my community, and had a chance to hear their stories. They inspired me as well. We all have challenges, and sharing our stories may inspire others to know they make a difference in their lives too.

***

I'm thankful Matt suggested we both go to a speaking conference to gain some knowledge about how to speak more effectively in front of an audience. Though we couldn't make speaking together work, I'm very appreciative of the opportunity to be asked to speak and share my story to audiences all over the country. Before my first solo talk, we had an opportunity to speak together.

When Matt was asked to speak at a restaurant franchise business conference and he asked me to come along and speak with him, I was a little surprised because we typically didn't do things together. However, I thought maybe this could be the start of something we could do well and have fun doing together. Even though our film crew came with us, we thought that since we'd been filming for a while, maybe I wouldn't notice they were even there and let them distract me.

We flew to Tennessee for the event. When we got there, Matt wasn't feeling well and told the film crew they couldn't film us then; they would have to go.

What? I wasn't sure what to do. Would he be feeling well enough to speak at the conference? I hoped he would be able to rally himself to speak, but we couldn't just stop filming everything. There was too much at stake in time and money with the crew.

So we ended up filming me sight-seeing in the area on my own while he rested. When I got back something still didn't seem right with Matt. His mood was drastically different, cold, and I didn't know why. He still wasn't feeling up to par, and we weren't sure if he could do his speech.

The next morning, he rallied himself and we went to the speaking engagement together, where we were introduced and Matt spoke first. He gave a good talk and was definitely in his element. I knew he would be; he's good at it. I was glad to be there with him. Then suddenly he ended his talk and just looked at me cold, like *Now it's your turn.* I was caught off guard. Was it my turn? There had been no lead-in, as we had discussed, to make a smooth transition from him to me.

Looking out at the audience, I got stage fright, and there was a long silence as I stood frozen, not knowing what to do. Eventually I managed to get through it. It wasn't my best speech, but I did okay. I was never so embarrassed; I had to hide back tears. I felt Matt had left me stranded up there. He didn't say a word when we were done, until later he did say he couldn't believe that I came with him to the event. He thought I should have turned him down and let him do it by himself.

Did I miss something? I was shocked. It didn't make sense. Why did he ask me to go, then? I didn't understand.

We didn't talk much on our way back home. Whatever happened or changed, I had no idea. I told myself I would not put myself in that position again. I was humiliated and didn't like the way he handled it and how it made me feel. We haven't done a speaking engagement together in public since.

After the trip with Matt, I wasn't sure if I could or would ever want to speak in front of an audience again. I was scared I'd freeze up on stage. Then, in 2007, an opportunity came for my first solo speaking engagement at the university I graduated from, Central Michigan University. Could I do this on my own? What was I going to speak about? The TV show? My experiences in college? I said yes to it because I wanted to see if I could do this on my own, at least once. We were still filming, so the production crew decided to come along and film since it was part of my journey of going out on my own. So a producer, a cameraman, and a sound person came with me. I was probably just as nervous having them there filming the event as I was getting up on stage and speaking. I was thrilled to be able to meet up with my parents and sister and visit with them the evening before.

The night of the engagement, I was nervous and scared that no one was going to come to this event and hear me talk. Maybe there would only be a couple hundred people, if that. Regardless of how many people showed up, this was an awesome opportunity for me and I didn't want to mess it up.

Then the memory of the talk I did with Matt crept into my mind. I couldn't let that get to me. *I can do this.* I was backstage getting ready when my producer came to see how I was doing. He asked me how many people I thought there were in the audience. The way he said it made me afraid hardly anyone was there, just as I had thought. Okay, maybe a couple hundred people or so? He said, "Not even close," with a big smile on his face. "Amy, there's still people waiting to get into the auditorium to see you, and about eighteen hundred people are already in the auditorium to hear you talk."

No way!

I didn't believe him, so I had to take a peek through the curtains to see if he was pulling my leg.

Oh my goodness. The whole place was packed, from the main floor to the balcony above. I couldn't believe it. It was overwhelming to see so many people at my first speaking engagement. But I couldn't walk away. I needed to do this, and I wanted to do it.

I clung to my notes as I walked out onto the stage. There was a step stool behind the podium so everyone could see me over the podium as I talked. But when I saw the audience I suddenly changed my mind and decided not to use the podium. Standing behind it felt too formal for me, and I wanted this to be more conversational if I was going to share my story about my life, the challenges I overcame, and what helped me to be the person I am now. Even though I had my notes, mostly for the sense of security they gave me, I didn't really use them. I was a nervous wreck the minute I walked out on stage as just me, myself, and I.

Once I saw everyone and started to talk, I knew I'd be okay. This was it. I had prepared myself for this and would do the best I could. The spotlight was shining on me, and I felt vulnerable, but as I began to share I also felt courageous and brave.

As I shared my story, the audience laughed at the funny things I said and were quiet at the serious stuff. Toward the end of my talk, I looked at my father and saw he had started to cry a little. I quickly turned away before I started crying too. The first time I ever saw my father cry was at my wedding. I wasn't sure why he was crying now, but afterward I found out it was because he had been worried about his little girl ever since I got married and moved away. When he saw me up on stage and heard me talk, he knew I was okay. He was so proud of me, at how far I had come, and what I'd accomplished. I had grown up and wasn't his little girl anymore. I was an adult, a mom, and I was going to be okay.

When I was done, something I did not expect happened: I received a standing ovation. I've been speaking ever since to various groups, sharing my story of hope, of believing in yourself, and that we all matter, have value, and a purpose in life. I did fantastically well for my first speaking engagement on my own, and I was proud of myself. To this day I typically don't stand behind a podium, and the response has been amazing because of it.

Just before my producer and I boarded our flight to head back to the farm, I mentioned something to him. As we sat down to eat, I apologized to him because I thought what we had filmed would probably be boring footage, not really useable, and that this trip had been a waste of time for them. I wanted him to see that I wasn't like Matt or like I pretended to be. I wasn't as dynamic, and I didn't over exaggerate or dramatize things like he did. However, this whole trip, including filming it, had been easy and kind of fun to do. It wasn't hard or agonizing at all.

Why didn't it feel this way when we filmed on the farm, instead of tense, chaotic, and often uncertain? Isn't this what reality TV filming should be like? Just simply telling your story, enjoying what you do, and hoping it's interesting and inspiring for others to watch? It didn't seem like that a lot of the time, maybe because of the toxic environment that had been created on our farm from the very beginning—"Do not trust the production crew."

I became different after that. It was hard to stay on board all the time to film, to appreciate what Matt was doing and what we were doing together as a family, because things seemed stressful, chaotic, mistrustful; like more of an effort to keep up our brand, our image, rather than just being ourselves. After that speaking engagement, I began to see our production crew in a whole different light. What we were doing didn't need to be hard. They were not the big, bad guys, but people I could enjoy working with.

It was a roller-coaster ride of emotions—one moment I thought we were okay, and the next everything seemed up in the air. I didn't quite know where I stood with Matt, on and off camera. Someone once told me that the person who creates chaos is usually the one who wants to be in control of it. I thought that was very interesting.

A Little Me

Because of our TV show, my family and I were able to go on some really awesome once-in-a-lifetime trips that we might not have been able to do otherwise, at least not in the way we did. I love traveling, and I'm grateful for those opportunities.

One of my favorite trips was the riverboat cruise down the Mississippi River on the "American Queen." It was wonderful to stop off at the small-town ports along the way, see the local areas, and visit with the people. My kids seemed to really enjoy it as well because it was like being Tom Sawyer and Huckleberry Finn cruising along on the river. We'd stay up late just sitting in the rocking chairs on the deck, playing checkers, and watching the sunsets. Riverboats are much smaller than the big cruise ships, and it felt more personal. We felt as if we had the boat all to ourselves.

After the cruise ended, my kids and I drove farther down south to work on a project for Habitat for Humanity (because of the flooding after Hurricane Katrina) and another project for a local charity. My kids learned a lot, and what an opportunity it was for them to help others and remind them of how fortunate we are. Our trip ended with visiting New Orleans.

Even though it was one of my favorite trips, it was also one of my worst, personally. We were in Memphis, Tennessee, visiting Graceland, when Matt suddenly said he had to leave immediately to take care of something back in Oregon at the farm.

What?

We had farm help there to take care of things. Did he really have to leave in the middle of our family trip? Yes, he did, and he left but said he would join up with us later. It left us up in the air as to whether we continued with the trip without him or not. We did continue on, hoping we'd see him later. The kids still had a great time, but I was worried about what was going on at the farm and how this trip was going to go, but I tried to have a good time as well. When he did meet up with us later at a port, the kids were happy to have him join us for the remainder of the trip.

Once Matt was back on the boat, several days before the riverboat cruise ended, he said we needed to talk. Out of the blue, he told me we needed to end the trip right then and go home if our marriage was going to be saved. Otherwise, it was over. I felt like I had just been punched in the stomach and couldn't breathe. If felt as though he was giving me an ultimatum without any discussion between us. And to do it here and now in this way was crazy and not right. Yes, I did know we had lots of problems in our marriage, but this was not the way to solve them. We could wait until we got home in a few days. We had a commitment and a contract to abide by as well.

I was scared, and my heart was pounding so fast; I didn't know how to respond right then and there. I wasn't sure what Matt was going to do. I tried to stay calm, and told him, "Let's finish the trip, and when we get home let's talk about our marriage, the two of us together, and what we both want and need to do to get it back on track." He didn't want to do that. He insisted we leave when we got to the next port, or our marriage was finished, over.

Why the sudden absolute? What about the production crew? We would violate our contract. And what would we tell the kids? Our marriage was my highest priority, but we also had a contractual responsibility to fulfill. We could talk about it and come up with a plan on how we would work this out when we got back.

However, at the next port, Matt got off the boat and left the kids and me behind. I put on a good front for my kids and for filming, but I was very uncertain as to what I would come home to. Would Matt be there or not? I was unsure. This was not exactly the first time he had done something like this. I was getting emotionally and physically drained, though.

As our reality show became a big success, going from one season to the next, and our farm business was growing well, my personal life was slowly falling apart. Many things around me were positive, but the most important personal thing in my life was not. Our little u-pick pumpkin patch was getting bigger; it was no longer a mom-and-pop u-pick stand but a farm business. We had to hire a few more farm workers and office staff to help us out. Our farm manager seemed to be doing a great job in her new position, from what I saw, and she was working a lot more with Matt in the office to make it all happen. I didn't interact a lot with our office staff or farm help. Matt wanted to take on the job of managing it all.

My kids were doing well in school and had a lot of good friends who were often at the farm. My son Jacob probably had the hardest time with the changes he saw in the family from filming our reality show. Practically Jacob's whole life had been on camera, as was most of Molly's and half of Jeremy and Zachary's. Jeremy and Zachary knew a little more about what life was like growing up on the farm before cameras were around. I didn't see how filming had affected Jacob's life until later.

During filming, I constantly reminded myself of my main priority: to be the best mom I could to my kids. I kept busy with my charity foundation, raising monies and speaking a lot around the country. Being a mom helped me stay humble, keep my feet planted on the ground, and be thankful for what I had and the opportunities we got. I wanted to do my best to make sure my kids' lives stayed as normal as possible and that I was always there for them, all while trying to keep my marriage together.

If I thought filming had a huge impact on my personal life, I soon had another thing coming. My life would be forever changed. Matt and I held ourselves together over the years filming our show because we thought it was good for the kids. If we could do that, then maybe when filming was over we'd give our marriage another chance. If I thought I was protecting my kids from what was going on in our relationship, I soon found out that was not the case—far from it. They already knew something was going awry—kids often do even when we think they don't.

As our business life grew stronger, we continued to grow farther and farther apart personally. I felt like the employees on our farm, the production crew, and others knew more about my life than I did. I think it was easier for Matt to manage it all so I wasn't in his way. Matt was spending more and more time at the tavern he often frequented in the evenings after filming and working on the farm, and our farm manager seemed to be around more and more often as well.

What, if anything, was going on?

Then it dawned on me. Matt and our farm manager, who had been working for us a number of years by then, seemed to have more than just a working relationship or friendship. I saw messages, pictures, and other things that should not have been shared between people who just worked together and were still married to other people.

I was devastated. I questioned what I was seeing; I wasn't sure if anything was really going on. I didn't want my imagination to run away with me and begin to imply something that wasn't true. Because if "nothing is going on," then I was crazy and thinking something I shouldn't have. If there was something going on, I felt like a big fool. Was I the only one who didn't know?

Foolishly, I said nothing and kept it all to myself. I stuffed my emotions deep down within me because I wanted to find out if what I had read and seen was true. And maybe I wanted to protect my kids and myself while I tried to figure out what to do. Besides, there was a big part of me that doubted what I saw, and what I knew. There had to be an explanation.

Because I didn't say anything, my emotions and attitude came out in other unhealthy ways. I took it out on Matt on camera sometimes instead of talking to him off camera, and that wasn't right. I cried a lot over those next several years. I didn't have a plan, and I didn't know what to do. Were Matt and our farm manager really in some kind of inappropriate relationship? What might I have done to cause it, if anything? I didn't even want to think about it, and began to shut down to try to deal with it.

In hindsight, I know I should have said something right away, but I didn't. I was scared and ashamed anything remotely like this could be happening. Was Matt really interested in someone else right in front of me? Why would he even go there when we were still married? Of course I knew our marriage was in big trouble, but I had hoped there was still a chance we could work it out when this big thing we called reality TV was over. If we could just hang on, maybe we could work it out. It just never seemed to end.

I kept quiet over the years. I didn't even think about divorce; I didn't want it to be an option. I've never felt so alone, hurt, and betrayed in my life. You don't have the option to look over the white picket fence to see what may be better on the other side before you take the time to see if things can be worked out and then decide if you want to move on. We got distracted—that I know—but you can't have it both ways. We could have, and should have, done more to make our marriage work, but it takes two to make that happen.

As we kept filming more episodes, we also kept doing more and more things separately. When we were together it was often tense. Then, just before Thanksgiving in 2013, Matt asked for a separation. In the back of my mind, I knew it was coming, but it was still a surprise and hard to accept. I was hoping our show would have ended at some point before this happened. I always thought there was possibility if we gave it at least one more try. He moved out into the double-wide house trailer we bought two years earlier for the other property we owned next door. He had it all furnished and decorated and ready for him to move in. When that had happened, I didn't know. Perhaps a little time away from each other would give us some space to figure things out.

About four months after we announced we were separated, my son Jeremy let me know he had proposed to Audrey and they were engaged. I couldn't have been more excited and happy for him. He felt bad about giving me such good news about his life, knowing I was going through a very tough time in mine. I told him not to feel that way. I didn't want him to worry about his dad or me, or have it affect his wonderful news. I was so happy he had found someone he wanted to spend the rest of his life with. His dad and I would figure it out and be fine. Zachary asked Tori to marry him about the same time as well. My boys were going to get married, and I was so happy for both of them!

I will always value marriage and all that it stands for. It *can* last a lifetime. My parents are an inspiring example—they've been married now for sixty-five years. But it takes two to make the effort to make it work. I just felt bad that, as parents, we didn't have a relationship that could be a model for our kids. Perhaps our relationship would serve as a lesson about what not to do.

Over a year later, at the end of January 2015, Matt filed for divorce. The year of separation went by fast, and we didn't have a plan to try to fix things. Even though I kind of knew it was coming, it was still devastating to me. I felt numb. I had hoped for a miracle, that it wouldn't get to this point, but now it was here. My marriage to Matt was over. Matt pushed to finalize the divorce in three months, but I didn't see that as realistic. How can you dissolve twenty-seven years of marriage in three months? How sad. I knew it would take longer than that, and I needed to find a lawyer. Our divorce became final in April 2016.

My personal turmoil was displayed on our reality show—it was a part of our story—but I made a promise to myself that airing it all on our show was not going to happen. It was not the place. I couldn't handle that. We were getting a divorce, we had our own lawyers, and when it became final, we received the divorce papers on camera. That was it. We both agreed that no details of it would be filmed, just a little about what we both thought personally. We were determined not to let this divorce turn into something mean and nasty. I did my best to put on a good front, but inside I was a mess.

Although I tried to manage this upheaval in my life as best I could, getting a divorce was like a living death to me. Something was lost, something died—our marriage—but you keep on going. There's a grieving period, which is different for each individual. Matt and I have remained cordial and respectful to each other, as we still film our show and currently manage to live on 108 acres together. We agreed I'd stay in the farmhouse and he would stay in the double-wide until we figure things out. It's hard, different, but we're trying to make it work for however long it makes sense. Our marriage may not have been able to be saved, but I'll do my best to still hold my family together.

I almost crumbled and fell after my divorce, but my faith kept me strong and hopeful. I knew God still had a purpose for my life and I still matter and have value, and that is my saving grace. Divorce wasn't going to be the end of me. It would be a start to a new chapter. It'll be hard at my age, and being a dwarf on top of that, to start life over again, but I'm choosing to not be stuck after divorce. I have no idea what to do or the direction my life will take, but it's a new start to something. My second act was about to begin, and I felt a little invigorated, and also guilty, about that.

Encouragement from Amy:

~It's okay to feel sad, mad, or however you may feel when things don't go right in your relationship, in your career, or with others. Give yourself a moment to feel that—it's important—but don't stay there. Allow yourself a day to vent constructively, get it all out, and then say, *Okay, enough. What's my plan?* Keeping feelings and frustrations all bottled up isn't healthy for you or anyone else. So allow yourself to vent and communicate with someone, and then move on.

CHAPTER 15

Second Act

Woohoo! My second act arrived differently than expected, but I was ready to go and live it. But first I had to get past being divorced, to survive the death of my relationship.

After many years I was finally in a place where I felt I could begin to live life again, only differently. Now what do I do, and what does it mean when I say I'm in my second act? It's about a new beginning, the start of a new chapter in a life already being lived. It's about where I am right now, continuing on, and at the same time starting over again. It's about overcoming many personal challenges and making it to the other side of the mountain still in one piece. It was getting to a place where I still liked myself and believed in my own worth.

Before and during my separation and divorce, I was in survival mode for a long time. While in that mode, I knew I was just maintaining my life instead of thriving. It's hard to thrive when you're only doing the bare minimum needed to survive. I was separated from Matt for just over a year, and our divorce took a year and a half to finalize. All that time, I was simply going through the motions, trying to hang on to my self-worth and confidence. I wanted to believe I wasn't all that bad, that I was still a pretty-awesome woman who still had a lot to offer and the ability to accomplish more.

Having come through this personal challenge intact was a big win for me. I know things could definitely have gone the other way, but I was determined to do my best not to go there or stay stuck in what was not to be. I wanted and needed to look forward to what was now new and different in my life.

I am proud of and thankful for what Matt and I did together, because, in the end, it changed my life for the better. We raised four great kids, and I'm so proud of each of them and the wonderful adults they have become, doing great things in their lives. And though we all had a part in making our farm successful, a lot of credit goes to Matt for the work he put into managing it over the years.

My second act is much different than I expected, but that doesn't mean it has to be less than what I hoped for. It will just be different.

So here I am, an empty-nester and a divorced, single woman. Just saying the words *I'm divorced* still takes my breath away sometimes. It saddens me that my relationship had to end. It was a living death, and there are moments I feel like I'm still grieving a loss. It was a loss, but it doesn't mean I stopped living. Marriage is important to me, something I didn't take lightly, and I still believe in it wholeheartedly.

Many have asked if I have any regrets. Absolutely. I could have done things differently, but we both did what we thought was the right thing. However, I'm glad I don't have the kind of regrets that would have kept me stuck in the mind-set of *if only . . . or should of, could of, would of* kind of thoughts. I did at first, but thankfully I got past that. I look with anticipation, as well as a little fear and uncertainty, to the days ahead, but I'm also hopeful. My second act is like a blank white canvas, and I get to choose how it will look. I'm planning to paint it with bright, joyful colors. I don't want to feel sorry for myself for what I lost, because that kind of thinking isn't going to help me move on in life, experiencing and embracing new things.

I've taken time to reflect on some of the things I've learned and how I've grown from my relationship with Matt. At first I felt like a complete failure at one of the most important relationships in my life. However, with failure, we need to allow ourselves to learn and grow from the experience and hopefully be a better person from it. Out of the sadness of divorce I've found the Amy I kind of lost. Even facing the uncertainty ahead, I feel I have a new confidence and a stronger trust in who I am, what I think, how I make decisions, and how I look at myself and others. I'm learning to communicate better and not shy away from having different ideas and thoughts from someone else. Boy, do I still have a lot to learn.

It would've been easy for me to have fallen into the trap of *Poor me, why me, where did I go wrong?* and to have overanalyzed everything I did or didn't do in my relationship. But I didn't.

Several years ago I came very close to being stuck in the mud of my past with that kind of thinking; I didn't know how to get out of it. Not only was it not fun, it wasn't very productive or healthy either. The fear of being stuck was much scarier than facing an uncertain future moving forward. I realized I can't keep falling into the trap of comparing myself to others, worrying about what I look like, about what others think or will say, and somewhere deep in my thoughts still thinking I'm not good enough. Enough was enough.

I'm in a healthier place now. My family and friends have always been there for me; I just needed to reach out to them. I regret keeping a lot of my thoughts and feelings to myself instead of expressing them in a constructive way. I regret that I was on the defense a lot instead of being more proactive. I regret building a wall around myself, thinking I could hide from being hurt and protect my emotions and heart, instead of confronting my feelings and expectations head-on. I regret being critical of myself and of those around me more than I should have, instead of appreciating others and myself more. I don't have to feel as if I'm in competition with anyone. I just need to be myself.

I regret that I felt alone when there were people around me who wanted to help and be there for me, but I closed them out. Cracks were showing, and I wanted to put myself together all by myself. It's okay to ask for help. Just by being there for me, nothing more, my close friends were a big part of helping me get through some tough personal challenges.

The glue that kept me together was my faith—always has been and always will. Even when I didn't think God was there, he was; I just didn't look to see that he was. I was too busy trying to fix everything instead of listening and allowing him to. In the second act I have in front of me are hope, possibilities, and faith. For that I'm grateful.

In the beginning it was hard, I won't lie. But as time goes on and things have settled down, the fog has lifted enough for me to see possibilities instead of a dead end. Having made it over the huge mountain that was in front of me, I'm kind of nervous and uncertain about what comes next, but I'm excited and looking forward to what I will make of this second act I have, as well. This opportunity is about finding out what Amy wants to do—where does my passion lie? How will I give to and serve others while staying true to my faith and self?

My house may be empty, but new life has entered my life, having kids who are married and having kids of their own, and becoming a grandma. Life is full of seasons; nothing stays the same. Like a tree in autumn, the leaves have to fall so new growth can come back and start over again in the spring.

Life may feel daunting, but at first everything does until you take a step forward. I'll admit, being on a new road at this point in my life and being a little person, figuring out my new normal, is a little daunting. But a challenge is upon me, and I'll rise to the occasion because I have a lot of life still to live.

I'm taking the time to reconnect and get to know myself, and to smile again at the many small moments that are happening around me. I am stronger for the challenges I've faced and overcome, and that encourages me as I look toward new adventures that await me. I'm stronger than I think, and I like myself more than I would have imagined coming out of divorce. I have a great community of friends and people around me who support and encourage me. I'm learning to let go so that new opportunities are able to come into my life.

My father's words from so many years ago still often float back into my thoughts: God doesn't make mistakes. My life continues to have purpose and value, and I matter. I'm grabbing life with open arms and an open heart of gratitude, appreciation, and love. What can stop me now? Only I can—my attitude and any roadblocks I put in front of myself.

Divorce is different for each individual going through it, and it's no different with Matt and me. His perspective about our life together is different than mine. We were both hurting in our own ways and reacted to it differently. It may have taken me longer to move past it, but I took the time I needed to start over in my personal and professional lives, and to make the decisions I needed to make, regardless of how long it took. I've been a stay-at-home mom for most of my life, as well as starting up a charity foundation and being a talent on our reality show. So starting over and supporting myself will be tough and not without struggle, but it won't be impossible.

Where do I begin? Whether I think life hasn't really changed much for Matt, personally or professionally, doesn't matter. Though Matt was an empty-nester like I was, his work and a personal relationship were already present in his life. I have some rebuilding and new construction to do in mine. Just acknowledging that to myself allowed me to get past focusing on where his life was compared to mine, and allowed me to see more possibilities for myself. I'm glad I've been able to move on and begin to rebuild my life.

When I turned fifty, there was one thing I wanted to do, something that would physically and mentally challenge me. I needed that at the time, and unbeknownst to me, it would help me down the road in what came next in my life—divorce. I was feeling stuck, stagnant, and needed something to change. I felt as if I needed to shake something up inside of me. My kids were either in college or living on their own, and my youngest was still at home finishing up high school when I decided I wanted to climb Mt. St. Helens.

Why climb a mountain? Because it fit what I needed to physically and mentally do to push myself and see something more. It was a daunting challenge because, physically, I was not even close to being in shape to take this on, and, mentally, could I handle the discipline it would take? Of course I could. I just needed to get in shape physically and mentally; then I'd be able to handle anything. I needed something to work toward so I could refocus and figure out where my life was going. I wasn't a stay-at-home mom anymore, I let go of my two part-time jobs years ago, my kids were grown up, and I needed to find something I would enjoy doing. Climbing this big mountain gave me a good start, as well as a kick in the butt.

I worked with a trainer several years before, but had taken a break from that kind of workout. Now I reached out to my former trainer, David, and asked if he would be willing to train me to get in shape to climb Mt. St. Helens. He said yes and, better yet, he would also climb it with me.

So we took the next four months to get me in shape. It was grueling at first. I hated that yucky feeling you sometimes get when working out, when you feel like you want to throw up, but David kept pushing me forward and I kept pushing myself. It's true: it's nice to have someone beside you to help you and root you on and make you accountable. I couldn't have done it without him.

Like the little blue engine that could, I kept telling myself, *I can do this. Yes, I can. Yes, I can. Yes, I can do this.* I kept going. I couldn't give up even though I wanted to many times. I could hear my father's voice in my ear saying, "Us Knights don't quit and give up. We find a way to keep going." Then you get over those initial few weeks of working out and your body begins to respond in a positive way to what you're putting it through and starts to give you the results you're striving for. Physical challenges remind me that nothing worth pursuing comes easy; it takes work, passion, and discipline, but it is well worth it. I was getting stronger, not only physically but mentally as well.

I invited Zach to come along on this adventure because I thought it would be awesome if we did this together. He was already in shape for it anyway. Perhaps I wanted a little moral support along as well. I was glad he said yes. Two little people, mother and son, were going to climb a mountain. I was getting more excited as the days got closer. We were still filming, as always, so our crew came along on this adventure too. This would be a big feat to accomplish, for two little people to climb Mt. St. Helens.

David wanted to give us a taste of what it would be like to climb Mt. St. Helens, but on a smaller scale, so we climbed Saddle Mountain in the Oregon coastal range, not far from my house. Though it wasn't bad, it was still tough, and I knew Mt. St. Helens would be more grueling and take everything I had to make it to the top. The week before we were to climb, we packed for the trip and David let us know what to expect. Unsure if we would be able to complete the climb in one day, he felt we needed to camp overnight at the base camp and then wake up early to finish the climb up to the top and get back down again before dark.

We got up early the next morning, just before sunrise, and got our boots on, put on layered clothing, and gathered our gear. As it got lighter, it was still a little cold in the morning, but it would get much warmer throughout the day. We couldn't have picked a better time to go. The weather was perfect—no snow, no wind; it looked like it was going to be a clear, sunny day—so off we went. We hit our base camp toward mid to late afternoon, set up camp, and had a dinner of dried food. It had been quite a while since I'd had dried food, and I must say, I'm not exactly a fan, but it was food.

Then off we went. The weather held up, with hardly any wind and the sun was shining. Before beginning the hike I reminded myself that my son was younger and in better shape than I was even though I had trained for this day. My trainer and his wife were also in better shape, and average size to boot, and their pace would be different than mine. My mission was not to keep up with them, but to find my own pace that worked for me to accomplish the challenge I set out to do—to climb a mountain, make it to the top, and then come back down again in one piece. Quitting was not even an option anymore.

We climbed, took rests, marveled at the breathtaking scenery along the way, and kept going. I climbed over big boulders that were just as tall as I was, if not bigger, as I tried to maintain my balance and footing over rocks, gravel, and ash. In 1980 Mt. St. Helens erupted and blew half of the other side of the mountain off, so we were hiking on an active volcanic mountain, climbing on ash and over rocks from that eruption long ago.

The higher we went, the thinner the air got, making breathing a little harder and slowing me down, but I kept going. *I can do this.* The closer we got to the top, the more excited I became at the thought of reaching it and what I was going to do when I did. *I will know when I make it to the top.* I kept my eyes on my climb, not looking up, afraid I still had a long way to go.

Suddenly, I was just yards away from reaching the top of the mountain. I was so excited I could hear my heart pounding harder and faster as I got closer.

Then I did it! I made it to the top with Zach, my trainer David and his wife, and with the whole film crew, who all cheered me on. I was speechless and in awe of what I had just done, and I was so happy I got to share the experience with Zach.

Seeing all the beauty around us was breathtaking. The air was so clear we could see some of the other mountains in the distance—Mt. Hood, Mt. Rainer, Mt. Jefferson, Mt. Bachelor, Mt. Adams—as well as the other side of Mt. St. Helens that had blown up. The mountain was still recuperating from the devastation that took place so many years ago, but it was beautiful to see some of nature's beauty coming back. Like nature, through life's hurts, losses, devastation, overwhelming odds, and feelings of uncertainty, beauty still lies underneath and fights to come back to thrive and shine again. Isn't that ironic?

Climbing Mt. St. Helens inspired me. No matter the tasks or challenges that lie ahead, I can and will overcome them. After my divorce and the changes that took place, I did what I needed to do, which was to pick myself up by my bootstraps, look straight ahead, and get going, believing I'm still worth it, instead of hanging around waiting for someone else to tell me that. I found a way to mentally, emotionally, and physically move forward. With what? I started off with hope, faith, and strength, and added in talent and intelligence too. This accomplishment helped me embrace the issues I needed to deal with after my divorce. When a door closes another opens up.

I wish my kids and I had never had to go through divorce, but in the end, I'm better and stronger for it and I know they will be okay. They still have a mom and a dad who love them, and my kids will always be the best thing we did together. I lost myself for a while, but now I'm back to figuring out who Amy was, is, and can be. Climbing Mt. St. Helens was like my life: there were lots of personal challenges to overcome and successes to celebrate, and with belief, I could climb over them and make it. My life experience has shown me a different kind of beauty that comes from within and will always keep shining through. That's hope.

I think it's kind of funny that I'm just now living on my own for the very first time. I went from my family home to living with college roommates, to going back home after I graduated, to getting married and living with Matt and my family. I found it kind of weird yet exhilarating at my age, in my fifties, to be living by myself. I found that I like the quiet and being by myself. There is something refreshing and reflective about it. I did miss not having people around all the time like I was used to; I missed sharing my life with others. Having had parents and siblings, a husband and kids, a production crew, friends, and others living with or being around me for most of my life, it feels very strange not to have that now.

The good thing the quiet gave me was time to reconnect with myself and challenge me to reconnect with my friends and know I really can do life single. I'm relearning how to handle a lot of things that fall solely on me now, like earning an income, paying bills, business, and carving out personal time. Living on my own empowered me to take charge and make decisions, and learn how to balance life.

One thing I've learned is that life shouldn't be about business all the time. It's good to know how to balance your life between business and personal. I think it's essential. Too much of either one isn't a good thing. It benefits any individual and relationship mentally, physically, and emotionally. I don't want to wake up one day and find out I missed out on some things or that it's too late to spend time with people I care about. I can't get back time. Business—making money to put a roof over your head and food on the table—is important, I know, but having business rule all the time, over your family, your relationships, and yourself, isn't healthy. It's about creating and maintaining a balanced life. It's important to set goals and have some sort of plan, which you go over periodically. This is why journaling and keeping a calendar are important to me, so I can reflect on what I've accomplished and what I still want to pursue.

There's nothing like the circle of life to keep life exciting and interesting. My kids are grown and getting married, and my babies are having babies. *What in the world? Where did the time go?* It's been a blessing to be a grandma, and I love every moment of being one. It's fun watching my kids be parents. It has helped me appreciate what my second act will be—wonderful! I love being a mom, and I love being a grandma, if not more. I can't wait to watch my kids experience one of the greatest joys in life—parenthood. With the trials that happen in life, seeing a baby smile reminds me that the small, special moments like these are priceless and important not to miss. Life does go on whether you're on board or not. I'd rather do whatever it takes to be on board.

Family is still the most important thing in my life. My two oldest boys are now fathers. Zachary and Tori have a son, Jackson, and Jeremy and Audrey have a girl, Ember. I'm reliving this time in my grandkids' life again, and it's awesome. You forget so much, but how wonderful it is being a parent! I'm thrilled all of my kids are relatively close to each other and to us. They're experiencing something I didn't have when I raised my kids: having family around. The cousins will get to hang out with each other, and my kids will have their siblings around. There is something about having family close by that keeps a family together. It's a bond unlike many others.

I missed out on something not having family around, but I made a point to make the holidays special and celebrated birthdays big. We did a lot together. I tried to help them understand how fortunate they were to grow up on a farm, get outside their comfort zones, and give back to help those in need.

Regardless of what happened between us, Matt and I love our kids and grandkids, and we'll always be family. We've been able to remain cordial and respectful, and to coexist on the farm, going our separate ways. We're still parents to four great kids together, we own the farm properties equally, and now we're grandparents. Being a family will not change because we're divorced; it'll just be different. Where we live may change, but family will always be the most important thing to both of us. A new kind of life awaits me, and I can't ever give up on myself regardless of my circumstances and challenges. If need be, I'll kick my attitude in gear because God hasn't given up on me.

A Little Me

I never expected I'd date at my age. I just wanted to be happy and have good friends and people around me. I didn't need to complete myself with another person. I would have just liked someone to complement my life, as I would his. After divorcing I wanted to get to know Amy again and find out what I wanted to do before possibly getting involved in another personal relationship. Dating wasn't even on my radar at the time. I was just trying to figure out what my new normal would look like, being single and in my fifties. I was looking forward to reaching out and getting reacquainted with friends I hadn't seen or done things with in quite some time. This was all new to me, for sure. I wasn't expecting to meet anyone I would end up dating, let alone be in a relationship with. It was the farthest thing from my mind. I came with baggage—at least I thought so: I'm a little person, I have a family, I'm on a reality show, I'm divorced . . . I learned a lot from the mistakes I made in my marriage, and I didn't want to make the same ones again if I found myself in a new relationship. I was just happy I still liked myself and knew I still had a lot to give to someone else if that was to come into my life again.

We continued to film our show during and after our divorce. A big chapter had closed, and I had to figure out how to start a new one on TV. My storyline was, how does Amy move on?

I wanted to move on by getting out there and meeting other people. I liked having my friends, single and married, around me, and I wanted to get to know other people too. So I got together with a single friend of mine to see if she would help me put an event together to meet other like-minded singles. She thought this sounded great and agreed to help. Then she called another friend and asked if he would help out by asking a few guys if they wanted to come to an event we were planning. She already knew a few girlfriends who might be interested. If we could make this work, it would be a blast. No expectations; it was just about meeting other people. We planned a mixed wine-and-art event, which I thought would be a whole lot of fun.

I was very nervous about filming the event because it could affect everything. I knew about filming and what it takes, but did the others know what they were saying yes to? I didn't know. Perhaps it was another element that made the event interesting for others.

We invited five men and five women, who would be paired up as couples. Each person would paint half a picture, and when a couple's paintings were put together they would look like one complete painting, but done by two people. It made for great conversation to see how the paired-up couple worked together while drinking a little wine and trying to get to know one another. I was paired with a man who had a great sense of humor and made me laugh.

This event was just what I needed to get out and meet other people, to simply have a good time. I so enjoyed meeting everyone who came, and I hoped to see them again. Deb and I were pretty excited by how it went and the fun time everyone had. We wanted to put on something like this again.

If I wanted to reconnect with my longtime friends and meet other people, I had to make it happen and not just wait around for it to. I did just that—not only with friends but with my kids as well. I went to a lot of music events in town to hear local musicians play, I went to the farmers market and got to know others in my community, I went out with my girlfriends, and to art events and other things that interested me. I started inviting others to a monthly soup night from fall to late spring. People actually wanted to come, and I always had a table filled with interesting people and conversation. There's nothing like gathering around a table with others. I kept busy with my charity foundation because giving back was still important to me and I wanted to keep making a difference in kids' lives as best I could. I also kept up with my kids and all they were doing since they moved out. I looked forward to them coming over unannounced just to hang out, and getting to see my grandkids. I enjoyed that they still felt at home when they stopped by the farmhouse.

About a month after the wine-and-art event, I had a summer pool party and invited everyone who came to the wine-and-art event, my other friends, and my kids. It was a gorgeous summer day for a barbecue, and we went swimming, listened to music, and sang around the campfire at night. If this was remotely what single life was going to be like, I was going to love it because it's what I loved to do— entertain and gather people around the table for good conversation, good food, and good memories.

At the barbecue one of the guys from the wine-and-art event, Chris, came up to me and we started talking. He was tall and handsome, with his white hair. Unexpectedly, he asked me if I'd be interested in going on a motorcycle ride with him since I had mentioned that I had gone once before and loved it.

What? Did he just ask me to go on a motorcycle ride?

Of course I said yes. I couldn't wait to go on this adventure.

A few days later he called to ask what my inseam was because he wanted to see about making adjustments to the bike. He was thinking about me and wanted to be sure I'd enjoy the ride with him. When he came to the house, he told me he had made adjustments to the foot pegs on his motorcycle and put a pair up higher so my feet could reach them and I could enjoy the ride more. I was amazed he even thought of that. He had me right then and there, but I had to tell myself, *Hold on. This is just one ride with someone, not a date.*

I went out and got a leather motorcycle jacket, helmet, and some boots. I had to look the part, didn't I? Now I was all set to go on this adventure with him.

We rode up into the hills and on some back roads around my house. Then we stopped and had lunch before heading back. I had an absolute blast and hoped I would have a chance to go again. It was fabulous. To my surprise, it wasn't the last time I'd see him.

Although I definitely wasn't expecting to date after my divorce, I told myself to be open to the possibility if it came along. I wanted to make sure I was giving myself time to figure out my life before I put myself into a relationship that deservingly needed time and effort on my part. *What do I want to do? What is Amy all about? Who and what is my community of people?* I didn't want to jump into something too quickly without taking the time to look inside and make sure I know myself, riding through this chapter in my life now. So I began to be more proactive in my life and do the things I wanted to do. Why not throw myself a get-together with friends?

Later in the month I planned a fun party for my birthday by going out on a boat on the Willamette River with a few close friends. I invited Chris as well. I was kind of nervous asking him. Crazy, I know, especially at my age. Nervousness has often prevented me from taking action, but not this time. Chris couldn't go; he had another event that day, but he wanted to take me out the next day for my birthday. *How thoughtful and nice.* I looked forward to that date with him.

A Little Me

We had dinner overlooking a lovely golf course, and the meal was great, but even more, I had such a good time with him. That was our first official date, and I hoped it wouldn't be the last. And it wasn't.

We started to see each other more and more, going to summer barbecues and listening to local music in town. I met some of his friends and he met some of mine (you know the guy needed to meet my girlfriends to get their approval). I met his family on a snow-mobiling and camping trip, and he met my kids and my family in Michigan. We spent time doing all sorts of normal, fun, and exciting activities together.

And low and behold, surprisingly, he was okay helping me do what I do sometimes—being a part of my reality show just because I asked. I tried to make sure he knew what he was getting himself into when he said yes to that, but can you really prepare someone for what it means to be on a reality show? No, not exactly.

We went on road trips, went skydiving, and just sat around and had dinner and watched movies at night together. I remember telling a friend, "This just seems and feels so normal." Yet I didn't really know what normal dating was. I'd had a long-distance relationship with Matt, where we only saw each other about four times, and here I was, dating someone I saw all the time. I felt good that I could simply be myself with him without any expectations.

We've been with each other over two years now, just having a good time being with each other. Although I'm in no rush to make a commitment, I look forward to seeing where our relationship may go.

Amy Roloff

What I wasn't planning for or expecting, having a relationship, came into my life anyway, and it has been wonderful and has made my life so much richer, sharing it with someone I care about. Where did the time go? It has given me a sense of happiness and sharing I forgot I could have with someone.

I think it was unexpected for my kids as well, and I worried about how they would be impacted by it and feel about their mom dating. I know it will take time for each of them and be an adjustment for them, but I hope they will be okay with it in the long run. Divorce may have happened to me, but it impacted others around me as well. I wanted to give them space by not pushing Chris, or anyone else, on them too soon. Chris felt the same way because it wouldn't be good for him or us.

It was exciting and empowering, and gave me a sense of freedom to be able to let things go. Besides, I needed to in order to be able to move forward and look ahead to possibilities. Getting to know Chris and learning about his quirks and habits, what makes him smile and what's in his heart, only enriches my life and makes me want to share more moments with him in this second act of mine.

I'm in a good place now in my life. I was definitely worried and uncertain for many years leading up to my separation and after my divorce whether I ever would be again. I have a new normal now, a new season of life. I'm glad I hung in there and gave myself the time I needed to adjust to the big changes in my life.

I realized Matt and our farm office manager were more than just friends for a long time, and that was rough. But time can be a good thing if we use it wisely. Everything is now in the open, and I think it helped me move on instead of hiding and staying stuck. Was I hurt, almost crushed? Yes. Regardless of where I'm at or whether I'm in a relationship or not, I'm in a better place myself and can be happy for him that he still continues to be happy in the relationship with her. By letting it go and not thinking I wasn't good enough, that I failed, and all the other what-ifs and self-doubts I told myself, I allowed myself to step out of that and begin a new chapter in my life, a second act. Besides, there will be many events and gatherings we'll all be at with family, and it's best to embrace it and be good with it—for my kids, my family, and myself.

My second act is in full swing, and I'm excited about some new projects I have going on and my personal relationship. My online business, Amy Roloff's Little Kitchen, is off to a good start. I love sharing things that will get people back to enjoying being in the kitchen, cooking, and gathering around the table with good food and good conversation, creating memories with family, friends, and loved ones. I enjoy continuing to speak all over the country to various groups, organizations, and conferences, sharing my story that everyone matters and has value and a purpose. And of course there is almost nothing better than spending time with my grandkids and good friends.

A big decision still left to make is what to do about the farm. Do I stay, does Matt stay, do we both stay on the farm together because we still own it fifty-fifty, do I take a buyout, or do we sell it completely? This has been hard to think about since it's been the only home I've known for twenty-eight years. But I've taken enough time, and now I'm in a place to let go and make a decision. The farm will always have a special place in my life because I raised my kids here, but life will continue on.

Just as when a relationship has ended, time heals. It may not make us forget, but it heals. Life is good.

Four particular things, out of many, have been the biggest factors in helping me face and get past the challenges in my life.

The first is my Christian faith. I have always believed in what my father said to me so many years ago—God doesn't make mistakes. God hasn't given up on me, and neither should I.

Second is getting rid of what-ifs and focusing on what I *do* have control over: my attitude. A positive attitude builds up resilience because it takes practice. Life happens, but it's how we respond to it that counts.

Third is my community around me. Are they helping, encouraging, and supporting me in a good and constructive way, as I hope I'm doing for them, or am I allowing them to hold me back? Who you have in your community—family, friends, mentors, coworkers, acquaintances—does matter because where you put your heart and time has an impact. Your community tells others something about you.

And the fourth is I matter and have value and a purpose. *I still matter.* No matter the successes or failures I will have in my life, I'm important and I will *always* matter. I have value. I'm worth so much more than I give myself credit for, and I'll go after what's best and not settle for less. My value is not dependent on what or how anyone else thinks about me, but what and how I think about myself. I have a purpose, though my purpose has changed over the years—I'm still a mom but to adult kids; I'm no longer a wife but a single woman. I still have a purpose—to do my best, and to serve and give back.

A Little Me

As I shed the roles I've had for a while and try on new ones, such as being a single woman, an entrepreneur, a girlfriend, mom, and grandma, I have a sense of renewal in my second act. I'm looking forward to seeing where I will go in life.

Stay tuned.

Acknowledgments

A BIG thank you to the following people:

Lisa Dixon. I couldn't have written this book, let alone gotten it published, without you. You are not only a very good friend—in fact, my best friend—you also continuously keep me grounded, prod me on when I want to give up, encourage and support me in all I do, and let me vent to you about everything. You always keep it real with me—no fluff—and you're always giving and loving.

The team at Indigo River Publishing—Dan, Navid, Bobby, and everyone else—for helping me accomplish a big project and for their dedication, tireless work, encouragement, advice, patience, and willingness to publish my book and let me share my story.

My family—my sister, Kathie, my brother, Roger, and my late sister, Cyndi—for letting me be just me, and a sister, without even knowing it; to my brother for being my protector and always helpful; to my sister, Kathie, for being the sister I needed throughout my life—a friend, listener, and confidant—and for reminding me family is everything; and to both my sisters for letting me hang out with them all the time.

A Little Me

My parents, Gordon and Patricia, for showing me a perfectly imperfect marriage and relationship, and for making it work to stand the test of time by continuingly giving love, respect, diligence, commitment, friendship, sacrifice, strength, and faith to each other.

All the individual little people who have come in and out of my life for showing me to believe in myself and reminding me not to let dwarfism or life's challenges stop me but to keep living.

All my friends, past and present, who have played a part in my life and helped me be the person I am today. I appreciate your friendship and what it did to help me push myself.

CPSIA information can be obtained
at www.ICGtesting.com
Printed in the USA
LVHW082249070619
620609LV00006B/50/P